The BEAR'S EMBRACE

A TRUE STORY OF SURVIVING A GRIZZLY BEAR ATTACK

PATRICIA VAN TIGHEM

GREYSTONE BOOKS

DOUGLAS & McINTYRE PUBLISHING GROUP

VANCOUVER/TORONTO

Greystone Books
A division of Douglas & McIntyre Ltd.
2323 Quebec Street, Suite 201
Vancouver, British Columbia V5T 4S7
www.greystonebooks.com

Library and Archives Canada Cataloguing in Publication
Van Tighem, Patricia, 1958–
The bear's embrace

ISBN 13: 978-1-55054-875-4   ISBN 10:1-55054-875-1

1. Van Tighem, Patricia, 1958– 2. Bear attacks—Alberta—Waterton Lakes
National Park. 3. Grizzly bear. 4. Face—Wounds and injuries—Patients—Biography.
I. Title
RD523.V36 2000   362.1'9752'0092   C00-910790-8

Editing by Barbara Pulling
Copy-editing by Maureen Nicholson
Cover design by Val Speidel
Cover photograph by Susan Middleton and David Liittschwager © 1994
Text design by Val Speidel
Typesetting by Julie Cochrane
Printed and bound in Canada by Friesens
Printed on acid-free paper

We gratefully acknowledge the financial support of the Canada Council
for the Arts, the British Columbia Arts Council, and the Government
of Canada through the Book Publishing Industry Development Program
(BPIDP) for our publishing activities.

*This book is dedicated to
all of my family,
my children,
my beloved "Joe."*

"Our deepest fear is not that we are inadequate. Our deepest fear is that we are powerful beyond measure. It is our light, not our darkness, that most frightens us. We ask ourselves: 'Who am I to be brilliant, gorgeous, talented, fabulous?' Actually, who are you not to be? . . . We were born to make manifest the glory of God that is within us. It's not just in some of us; it's in everyone. And as we let our own light shine, we unconsciously give other people permission to do the same. As we're liberated from our own fear, our presence automatically liberates others."

— NELSON MANDELA

"Why should we give up the dream of embracing the bear?"

— TERRY TEMPEST WILLIAMS

Contents

Author's Note

The names and identifying details of some characters and places have been changed to preserve anonymity.

I

The Hike

The sky is clear and blue, blue. The trees are yellow. The air is crisp, cool, full of autumn sunshine. I am content riding along in our little blue Volkswagen Rabbit with my hand on Trevor's knee. We are headed south on Highway Two to Waterton Lakes National Park.

Trevor hums under his breath, and I look over at his bearded profile. I am uncertain if we've made up after our disagreement last night. He planned to go rock climbing one day this September long weekend, maybe do a hike with me the next, but I wanted us to spend all three days together, backpacking. We haven't hiked for such a long time.

Last night I sulked in the rocking chair, tipping myself

abruptly back and forth. "I'll go alone, then," I said. Trevor sat in a calm pool of lamplight across the living room, his bushy dark head bent over a textbook. "I need to get away somewhere this weekend." He kept his head down. "Trevor!"

"I'm listening." Then, opening his arms, "Come here." I moved to the big armchair and sat on his knee. "All right," he said. I felt his sigh on my neck through tangled hair. "We can try out our new tent."

We enjoyed packing up. Trevor went out at the last minute for groceries and brought back all of my favourite backpacking junk foods. Now he's singing beside me in the car. I love his voice. On one of our first dates, we went out Christmas carolling, and hearing him sing then strengthened my determination to hang on to him. He looks over and smiles.

"Hi, my love."

There are shorn yellow fields on either side of us. Farmhouses dot the little gravel roads that run off from the highway. In the distance, the mountains show clear in the late afternoon light. Trevor and I have escaped to those mountains many times since we met five years ago. We used to get away to hike or ski or ramble almost every weekend. But recently, with both of us working shifts, it's been hard to organize time away. I settle into the seat and close my eyes, enjoying the warmth of the sun. Trevor gives my hand a brief squeeze.

"This was a good idea, Trish," he says. His voice is teasing, daring my "I told you so" to pop out. I don't rise to the bait. I can hear him laugh.

Trevor is still wearing his good pants and sports jacket. He's in his third year of medical school and partway through his pediatrics rotation at Children's Hospital in Calgary. I'm a nurse. I don't know if I feel like one yet, though I graduated a year ago and have worked since then on a busy surgical floor. I find it frustrating and difficult. There are many cancers and deaths to deal with, and not enough time to give patients the attention they deserve. I want to give this weekend my all and shake off the tense Patricia, leaving the pulls and pressures of nursing behind.

Trevor and I will stop in the little foothills town of Pincher Creek for supper, then stay tonight at a lodge in Waterton. We've left our plans for tomorrow wide open. We'll wake when we want to and take our time with breakfast and discuss where we'd like to hike. We're driving into dark storm clouds now, and a spattering of rain hits our windshield. It's strange how fast the weather can change.

❧

On a hot evening a week before our hike, I stand facing the mirror that stretches across the counter in our Calgary bathroom. The room has the cheap beige countertop of student housing, and cheap beige flooring. There is a green-and-black framed print on the wall, "Recipe for a Happy Marriage," received as a gift at our wedding three years ago. I'm in my white nursing uniform, a shift just completed.

I am twenty-four. My hair is blonde and brown, like a taffy pull. My teeth are well aligned after teen years in braces. All my life, I've been told that my blue eyes are lovely. I think so too, shy approval coming from deep inside. My nose would be better if it were smaller and straighter. My mother's nose. My grandfather's nose. I smile at myself just to see how I look. Some people have such marvellous smiles, smiles that wash over you and warm you. I wonder if my smile is like that. Trevor says it is. So does my mother.

I'm proud of how I look, but I struggle with that pride. As a Catholic, I've been taught that pride is a vice. Not good. Not right. I remember how my instructor would wring her hands in ballet class. "Such proportion, such legs. If you would only stand up tall! Look proud!" A small part of me was flattered. A little smile would come, but I could never allow myself to take her words to heart. It is easier now that Trevor adores my tallness.

"What are you doing, Trish?" Trevor calls. "Come to bed."

"Just changing. I'm coming."

I unzip my uniform and let it fall in a puddle at my feet. I stand tall and slim and fit in bra and panties. My eyes linger for a moment on my unblemished body. My patients have had breasts removed, tumours investigated, bowels totally resected. I hug myself and shiver.

I flick off the light and pull on an old flannel nightie, blue, with no softness left in the fabric. Trevor calls me again. He has turned his reading light out, done with studying for tonight. He's preparing for exams, squeezing his reading in between classes and labs and tutorials and hospital ward rotations. He likes children, loves the time he spends in pediatrics. "Can your husband come out and play?" our little neighbour Jason asks me whenever he sees our front door open.

"Did I take too long? Are you asleep already?"

"No, I'm still awake. Barely."

"I can't stop thinking about work," I say, climbing into bed. Trevor puts his arm out and draws me to him. "I'm glad I'm changing floors. If there were more of us in surgery, more nurses, we would have time to really care for our patients. It drives me nuts. There's a woman in now who had a breast removed for cancer. She's only thirty-eight, and they did a radical mastectomy. She has a scar from her chest to her shoulder and a lot of pain. We should be able to sit with her, hold her hand when she's crying, but instead we only have time for the basics: check her dressings, empty her urine bag, empty the drain under her incision."

Trevor rolls onto his side and kisses my face over and over. "You are a very good nurse. You get all the things done that need doing, but you give the other stuff, too. All you have to do is smile at a post-op patient, and you lighten her load."

I whisper into the dark. "There's something else I wanted to talk to you about."

"Mmph."

Trevor's breathing is becoming slow and regular.

"I'm working shifts and you're working shifts and we get so grumpy with each other sometimes," I say. "I want us to make it. Remember how we promised to grow old and wrinkly together? I want that to happen."

There's no answer, and I curl myself around my sleeping husband. When I close my eyes, I see visions of scars. In addition to two people with bowel resections and three women with mastectomies, my patients right now include two people who've had their gallbladders out and one who received an emergency appendectomy. My last shift passes through my mind as though on a screen. Me trying to answer three patients' bells that have all gone off at once. Two people want painkillers and the third has a leaking incision drain. I hurry to change his linens and redo the dressing, knowing that two other patients are waiting at their bedsides for me to help them finish up their morning wash.

I push the images from my mind, rolling away from Trevor. I will talk with him in the morning about getting away. We will do something together.

Crypt Lake Trail sounds like a wonderful hike. According to our guidebook, it's only about five miles long, but we'll gain two thousand feet. We have to take a boat trip across Waterton Lake to reach the trailhead, and there's a tunnel through a rock area somewhere along the way. The trail should satisfy the adventure needs of my kayaking, mountain-climbing, glacier-skiing husband and provide a challenge for me, his cautious wife.

The day is sunny and clear, but the wind off the lake is cold, and we've got our coats zipped up to the top. The lake stretches miles away to the right, with steep mountains on either side. The evergreen forest is mixed with deciduous trees that give it a blast of autumn colour. It's difficult to believe that it's supposed to snow tonight. Trevor wonders if I wouldn't rather stay at the lodge again tonight, but I want to backpack our gear in and camp.

"That's what we're here for, isn't it? We can snuggle up together. It will be fun." I'm happy and full of energy as we wait to board the boat. Bundled in his sweater and pile jacket, Trevor wraps his arms tightly around me for a feet-off-the-ground hug.

The trip is choppy and chilly, with people packed around us on the open wooden seats. The boat drops us at a crude wooden dock with two other hikers, then chugs off to continue its sightseeing tour of the lake. Dark green trees surround us, crowding the narrow shoreline and rising steeply from the water.

We adjust our packs and set off at an easy pace, talking and teasing and laughing our way up the gradual switchbacks. The other two hikers have disappeared with purposeful strides ahead of us. The water is far below us now, mirroring the cloudless blue of the sky.

"Hold on a minute, Trevor. I want to get a photo of you against the lake and the mountains on the other side."

"It won't work. If you focus in on me, the other side will just be a blur of colour."

"I want to try. The sun is so bright. It would be a good picture." Looking through the viewfinder, I see Trevor tilting his head and putting on a fixed smile.

"Trevor!"

"What?"

I am laughing, imitating him. "In every picture we have of you, you're tilting your head and smiling that tiny smile." Trevor laughs too, his face clear and happy in the afternoon light. Click.

"That was *much* better." I jump aside quickly to avoid Trevor's grinning lunge. He dives for me and we struggle, tickling each other through our bulky outdoor clothes. The ground beneath us is rocky and hard, cushioned in places by fallen aspen leaves. Then the trail climbs sharply uphill, into thick evergreen growth, and all of a sudden I feel apprehensive.

"Come on, Paranoia Pearl. Quit looking for bears at every corner, and let's go."

"Let's sit for another minute. That hill looks awfully steep."

We haul ourselves onto a large rock.

"Remember how we met? I can't believe it's only been five years." I pick up a branch of pine needles, caressing it to release the scent. "I feel like we were meant to be together. We're incredibly different, but we want so many of the same things. A house with a bay window. Babies. Taking our children backpacking, when we've got some. I sure hope we're not one of those couples who can't have kids."

Trevor's hand comes up to stroke my cheek. High above us the wind pulls at the tops of the pines.

I was just home from an exchange program called Canada World Youth when Trevor and I first met in 1978. Four months in the Ivory Coast, then back to the culture shock of Calgary. During a visit with friends from my African group and people who had been with Canada World Youth in Guatemala, we planned a get-together, reviewing a list of participants to phone. Trevor's name leapt out at me, as though it was the only name on the paper. I couldn't stop asking questions about him. Later, our paths crossed at a debriefing meeting for the Calgary-area participants. In a tiny front hallway jammed with winter coats and boots, we squeezed past each other, belly to belly. He was arriving. I was leaving. He went inside and asked about me. I went outside and asked about him. Who was the tall, blue-eyed blonde? Who was the dark-haired man with such wonderful eyes?

That's Trevor Janz, my friends told me. The name on the list. I was amazed.

"We'd better get a move on," Trevor says now. "That climb ahead of us isn't going to go away."

With a parting kiss, I step ahead of him onto the narrow trail, nodding hello to a family of four on their way out. We hike until we reach Burnt Rock Falls, halfway along the trail. There Trevor steals the camera out of my pack while I crouch to retie my long red bootlaces, and takes my picture. Our disagreement of Thursday evening seems long ago.

We stop again, farther along the way, at a jumble of enormous fallen boulders. The sun is being threatened by towering grey clouds, and it is cold as we sit finishing our snack. A low rumble from up the trail gets louder and louder, and soon a colourfully clad line of children traipses past. There are about twenty of them and a few adults, all wearing small daypacks.

"Where are you from?" I call loudly above their din.

"Red Deer!"

They vanish as quickly as they appeared, and Trevor and I are alone again.

It's uphill from here. We walk quickly to get warm; the sun is gone for good today. The view is incredible, with mountains all around us and hundreds of feet of waterfall far across the valley. We puff our way up steep switchbacks.

I stop. I can smell something for a minute, then it's gone. It's unpleasant. I think of bears.

"Trevor, can you smell that?" Silence surrounds us. We stand sniffing into the wind.

"I don't smell anything. Wait. Now I do." Then it disappears again. Trevor shrugs. "It's probably just that plant that gives off a pungent odour when you kick it. I can't remember what it's called. I don't see any bear scats."

With a glance up the trail, he strides away. I stand another moment and gaze around me. It doesn't look like bear habitat here, in such a narrow rocky valley. The scrunch of Trevor's boots on the loose gravel trail is getting faint, and I hurry to catch up, the smell forgotten.

At the campsite, a kitchen shelter sits between widely spaced spruce trees. We leave our packs there and continue up the trail, crossing a creek and following the rocky path across grey scree. Ahead of us, through massive, dark rock slabs, a tunnel stretches for about twenty feet. We move through it on all fours. I don't like the feel of rock pressing so closely on all sides of me, but I hold still for pictures, then scurry to the end and the open mountainside. Trevor lingers, examining the walls and musing about how the tunnel was formed.

Crypt Lake is still and quiet, with high peaks encircling it on three sides. Dirty patches of snow on scree slopes merge with deep waters. The sky is low and heavy, with dark cloud shadowing the mountain and lake. I shiver. The hike up here was more exciting than this. Turning, I see the blue of Trevor's jacket wandering down the shoreline. I lie flat on a limestone slab to escape the wind, closing my eyes to listen to the silence. But I can't relax with the cold seeping through me. Trevor's returning footsteps and his voice are welcome sounds.

"Let's go and cook us some supper, wife." He offers a hand to pull me up. "This is great up here. Over that mountain is Glacier National Park, in the States. We're that close."

"Uh huh." I look up at him. "I'm freezing."

We set up our new bright-green "worm" tent away from the shelter, then take a few minutes to rig a food cache high between two trees. The two other hikers we met on the boat have an enormous fire going in the shelter. We talk over supper and share some burning sips of Southern Comfort as the sky darkens. Big, soft snowflakes whirl and dance behind us. Trevor and I sit close, warding off the chill.

A white world greets us in the morning. Tiny crystal flakes are falling. Still in our down sleeping bags, we treasure a last few moments of warmth. I am tucked under Trevor's bearded chin, where I listen to the steady, slow beat of his heart.

We can hear the voices of the other two campers and the beginning crackle of a morning fire. If we want to catch the morning boat back to town, we need to get moving. Reluctantly, I release Trevor. He dresses and clambers out of the tent, disturbing my warm calm. The cold of the day steals into my sleeping bag no matter how tightly I seal it around my head and neck. I sigh. Time to get up.

I put on every piece of clothing I brought, but I'm still chilled through. Trevor is full of smiles and loud song.

"Get to work; you'll warm up then," he jokes.

I ignore him. The pit fire at the shelter is strong, but it warms only a piece of me at a time. Trevor pulls out frozen pita bread, frozen peanut butter and frozen oranges. He suggests we thaw them, but I have no patience to wait. I take a quick, tongue-burning sip of his tea and a handful of trail mix from the open bag on the table, then stuff my fingers back into heavy mitts and shoulder my pack. Trevor will do the last few minutes of packing up.

I am glad to be alone in this Christmassy world. Mine are the first tracks to mar the fresh snow. My breathing and the swishing of my clothing are the only sounds. It's nine o'clock, according to the other hikers. The boat won't be at the dock to pick us up till eleven-thirty, so we can take our time. Happy and warm now, I plod along in solitude.

Soon Trevor crunches up behind me. There is snow in his beard and all over his tuque. Even his bushy eyebrows are coated with flakes. He sails on by, calling me a slowpoke. I give him a quick shove as he passes.

"Are you warming up yet?" he calls over his shoulder.

I yell back. "Are you kidding? It's hot out here. I need to stop and take my coat off!" He smiles and waves.

The narrow valley stretches dark green and white ahead, with soft grey cloud close above. What a contrast to yesterday's early brightness. Trevor's blue anorak and orange backpack move brightly ahead of me. He waits at the steepest parts of the trail to give me a hand. As we descend, he describes some of the geomorphology of the area. I'm only partly listening, caught up in the exhilaration of the wintry mountain morning.

It doesn't take long to cover this part of the trail. We are already at the bottom of the big elevation gain, with the boulders where we passed the kids from Red Deer in front of us. There is such an abrupt change here from open rocky slope to thick forest. In a minute, we will be in the trees again. I hear the tramp, tramp of our boots on snow and gravel. The sound of Trevor's singing up ahead makes me glad. "Blue skies smiling at me, nothing but blue skies do I see . . ."

He's gone around a bend now and is obscured from sight by trees. I quicken my step to rejoin him. The trail has widened, and we could walk beside each other, hold hands and talk.

A bear.

And Trevor.

Two more steps forward. I stop. A bear? From the side. Light brown. A hump. A dish-shaped face.

A grizzly. Charging. And Trevor. Fast. He half turns away. The bear's on him, its jaws closing around his thigh, bringing him down.

Seconds pass. Time holds still.

A grizzly?

I take two steps back. Where am I going? What should I do? My heart beats loud in the silent, snowy woods. I can't outrun a bear. It knows I'm here. I can't leave Trevor. Panic rising. How will I get past the bear? Trevor? My mind racing. Legs like jelly. Shaky weak. Think.

The bear has Trevor. I can't see anything because of the bushes. I can't hear anything.

Not a bear!

I can't run. Take off my pack. It might divert the bear. After summers of handing out "You Are in Bear Country" pamphlets at the Banff Park gates, instructions for a bear encounter flash through my brain. I throw my pack down. So fast. My mind whirling.

Climb a tree.

Grizzlies can't climb trees. Nor can I! I have to. A tree with small, dry branches all the way up, right beside me. Get up! Steady and slow, shaking. Don't fall. Don't break the branches. They get smaller the higher I go. I have to stop. I feel very high. The branches are thin. Can't go higher. Stop climbing. Look down.

Trevor?

Scared. Snow falling. Soft. Absolute quiet.

I freeze. Terror fills me. It's right there. Eye contact. Small bear eyes in large brown furry head, mouth open. It's charging the tree. A scream, loud. It's moving so incredibly fast. It can't. Grizzlies can't climb trees! Everything so fast. It launches itself at the tree. Three huge lunges, branches flying and cracking. Twenty feet up. I'm frozen. Up. Brown ball of muscle and fury. So fast. Another scream. Cut off. Knocks the branch out from beneath my feet. Swats at my leg. My mind folds in.

On the ground. What's happening? Protect my head. Which way is up? Roll on my front. Play dead, and it will go away. It will go away. Trevor and I are not supposed to die yet. Don't fight, make it worse. Be passive. Hold still. Tuck my chin in. I won't die. It will leave.

A grizzly is chewing on my head.

Crunch of my bones. Slurps. Heavy animal breathing. Thick animal smell. No pain. So fast. Jaws around my head. Not aggressive. Just chewing, like a dog with a bone. Go away! I'm holding still. Horror. I can't believe this. Scrape of teeth on skull. Which way is down, so I can put my face there? Slurping and crunching. Lolling my head in its jaws. Playing with my head.

I'm angry.

I don't want to die. Get lost, you stupid bear! My mother will be so sad. I don't want to be a tragic death. Everyone will cry. Thoughts flit through my head. Incredulous. Angry. Terrified. Helpless. The bear is doing so much damage. Crunch and scrape. Anger wants to explode from my head. I don't want to die.

One hand pinned under my head. Work fingers free. There's a huge, distorted black nose right there in front of me. My fingers reach to tweak it. Gently. A diversion. Don't want to make the bear more angry. Big and black and sensitive, like a dog's nose. Divert it from chewing on me. A light twist. Blurred view. Don't look now. A woof! It's backed off. Am I dead?

Open an eye. Peek. It's still there, pacing in front of me. Walks ten feet, turns. Swinging its head back and forth. Ten feet and turns. Looking at me. Low woofs. Little eyes, looking right at me. Quick, close my eye. Perfectly still.

Please God make it go away.

Please God make it go away.

Please God make it go away.

Over and over in my head. How long?

The bear is gone. Absolute silence. Am I dead? How can I tell? I'm breathing. I hear it. Alive. Now what? Very, very cold. Head cold. Head wet. Warm wet, turning cold. Ground hard. Hold still. Don't move. Where is it now? Play dead.

Trevor?

No pain. Head feels strange. Shivering. Now what? Need to get warm. I can't see. Grope for my pack. Right there. I want the sleeping bag. Fumble. Too weak. A jacket. My pile jacket. Lie and wait. Rest. Scared. What do I do? Panic rising. Stay calm and think. Those two hikers. They'll be coming. Wait.

Trevor?

In the absolute silence, I try to call him. Panic. I can't pronounce his name. Why? My mouth? Don't think. There's no answer. Silence and cold. All so fast. I drift.

How much time before distant voices sound? There they are. The other hikers. Getting louder. Sound of footsteps tramping on snow. Time distorted. Spinning. I am crying, trying to stand, to talk. Help us, let's go, crying, afraid, head floppy and strange, shoulder sore, can't see.

Loud voices. Terror in the voices. All of us. Trevor's voice too. Hard to understand him. I can't see. Shouting. We'll go for help. No! Take us with you. Away from here. Before it comes back. Get us out of here. On hands and knees, groping. I'm blind, but I'll crawl this trail if I have to. Can I stand? Have to walk. Have to get out of here. Shouting. I'm standing. Cold and wet and weak, joining in the yells.

"Someone take my arm. Take my arm! My arm!" Voices far away, then louder again. Someone takes a gentle hold of me. Mind fuzzes in and out. Let's go. Get out of here. Where is the bear?

I'm shaking. A sleeping bag is placed over my head gingerly. Encases my head. Don't think about it. Warmer. Wrapped around my shoulders. My shoulder hurts. Don't touch that arm, whoever you are. The other side. Let's get the hell out of here.

Head strange. Like Medusa, flopping. Stumbling, the ground rough. Three miles at least. Couldn't just lie there. The bear would come back and drag me into the bush and bury me, like they do. No way. Not me. Hard to walk. Weak. Want to slip away. Can't. Walk. The other hikers yelling. Scared. Yelling. To scare the bear away? Is it back? Oh God. No, it's not. Heart pounding. Someone helping me. He walks fast. Panic. Can't keep up. Fall. Can't get up. A hand under each armpit and heave. Where are my feet? Stand. Keep walking. Pain. They take turns. Trevor? Where are you? He is far ahead of me with the other guy, loud voices receding.

"Trevor!"

Don't leave me. Stay close. I can't see. I can't walk any faster. I can't walk any more. Are we close? It's uphill here. My heart threatens to stop. No breath left. Another yelling decision. I yell too. Make a stretcher from the sleeping bag. Try. Can't. Agony to lay my head down. World spins, spins. Piggyback. Coat around my head to calm the snakes that flop. Shoulder hurts. Uphill piggyback. Dead weight. Can't stand it. Put me down.

Slip away.

Voices. They want us to wait. They will go for help.

No! I can't. Don't want to die. We'll get there. We'll make it to the boat. Help me walk. Walk, legs! Trevor's voice is strange. Garbled. I saw him for one upside-down and bloody moment. Can't see now. Another mile, they call. Downhill. Stumbling. Hold tight to the arms holding me. Walk. Trevor's voice. We'll miss the boat. He's going to run ahead. He's gone.

No! Stay, Trev! Stay!

The yells are less frequent. My helpers breathe heavily on either side of me. We're just about there, they say. I'm doing great, they say. Under-the-breath curses, mutterings. Frightened. Incredulous. Just keep walking. For the first time, I know where we are. A log across the trail to climb over. I remember this from yesterday. Not much farther. Relief washes through me. I am only partly here. Can't think. Head strange. Hurts. Slow and steady. Talk to myself. Keep walking. Cold. The wind colder now.

Wind off the lake? Are we there? Please.

Don't think. Just walk. Almost there. Another voice. Other footsteps.

"I'm Jim." Calm and steady. "I'm a paramedic."

Sink. The ground meets me. I'm gone. Safe. Help.

I'm moving. I hear water. Slapping. Splashes. Climb into a pitching boat. Don't anyone touch me. A snowstorm. So cold. See nothing. Black world. Night? Voices rise and fall around me. The world sways and swings. Wedge myself against a corner, the boat motor loud. No one touch me. Hurt. Wrapped in something. We'll get there. Safe now. Voices compete with the motor and the wind. Good. Bear can't get us now. Hold on. Don't slip away. Don't die. Boat slams against the waves, bucks and rises. Travelling fast. Wedged, hold perfectly still. Blackness. Hurt.

Some kind of bench. Where am I? Strong male voices with German accents. Gentle hands. Want to take a look. Blood pressure. A doctor. They'll take me to the local hospital, where Trevor already is. Mummified. Slow motion. Take care of me. Is Trevor okay? Yes, he'll be okay, they tell me.

Into a vehicle. Sometimes I'm here, and sometimes I'm not. Want me to put my head down. No! Don't touch me. Fight with strong arms. Want me to relax, put my head back. Can't! Let me hold it myself. Don't touch my head. I win. Feel the big body next to me. Shivering violently. How far? I want this to be over with. The ride is bumpy. Pain. Safe.

Emergency-room sounds. Is it over now? The accents and big men are gone. Footsteps. Sense of bright lights. Shivering fiercely. Don't let me fall off. Am I lying on a stretcher? My head feels strange. In pieces. A warm hand holding mine. Puff and hiss of blood-pressure machine. Starting an intravenous. A friendly voice. Each hand? IV morphine. Doctors introduce themselves. Contact. Calming. Relax.

"How's Trevor?" Lips strange.

"He's fine. He's right here. We're going to send you both to Calgary as soon as we get you fixed up."

Blackness bundled inside of me. Afraid again.

Going to cut your clothes off. Put big hot-water bottles all around you. Wrap your head with dressings. Warm you up. Morphine fuzz, in and out. Don't hurt. Just drift. Shaking. Don't let me fall on the floor. Warm around me. Cold inside. Head feels big. Pain fuzzing.

"Trevor's okay?"

"He's fine. He's right here."

Papers flipping, footsteps to and fro, carts, machines. Warmer now. Oxygen to breathe. Shivering. Drift. Safe here. No bear. I won't die. We won't die.

In the ambulance, I'm baking with the hot packs. Still shivering. They are so heavy. Can't move. It must be night by now. So dark. The attendant has a female voice. Take these things off me. She won't. Not yet.

"Is your head sore?" More morphine. Drift.

I have to pee. Try the bedpan. Can't. Laughing. Can't pee. So funny. Time twists around me. Patricia way inside me, laughing. Floating.

Calgary. We've slowed down. Oxygen on. Foothills Hospital. Good. They'll put in a few stitches, and we can go home.

Emergency. More sounds. More bright lights. Can't see. I'm scared. Noisy all around.

"How's Trevor? I have to pee."

"He's doing fine." The hand warm and reassuring, holding mine. A catheter and relief. It's so dark. Hurting. Not me.

"We're going to call your parents now."

A male voice. A flurry through my head. Call my parents? No! They will be so upset. Don't. Have to. A bear. Oh God, no. I want to scream.

Up. X-ray. Trevor's mother says hello. She's crying. Can't see her. Above my stretcher. Why is she crying? We'll be fine, Sarah. We're safe now. I smile under my bandaging. Reassure her. Drift.

Another male voice. "We're taking you to the operating room." Me? "We might have to do a tracheotomy."

I'm moving. On a stretcher. To the OR? In and out. No way! I don't want a trach. I can breathe. I can talk. But what's wrong with my face? Panic engulfs me. No no no. Drift away. On the stretcher.

II

The Hospital

Eileen Van Tighem (mother)

The morning is dreary. Overcast. It is a Sunday, and as we ready ourselves for Mass, I am restless. I feel that something is wrong, but I don't know what. At church I am agitated. My husband, John, is sharp with me. "Sit down!" he whispers. I can't. I go to the back of the church.

At home, we don't have long to wait. The phone rings. It's a doctor from the Foothills Hospital Emergency Department. Patricia and Trevor have been in some kind of accident. We call the Precious Blood Sisters. They will offer their prayers.

On the drive through yellow trees, up the busy Crowchild Trail, we question. Where? How? Why? Through the glass sliding doors, then into a small waiting room. The emergency doctor comes to see us.

"It was a grizzly bear," he says.

Oh God!

"You can't see her. She's going in for surgery."

Alone in the little waiting room, we are in shock. A young student nurse comes in and sits beside me, holding my hand.

Hours and hours and hours of waiting. Trevor's mom and family, John and I. Waiting and waiting for the surgeries to end. Trying to keep each other's spirits up. Someone tells us that Trevor had yelled across the emergency room, through his bandages, "Trish! How are you?" and that Patricia had yelled back, "I've had better days!" We laugh. A nurse reprimands us.

At last, Patricia is back. She is alive.

Her head is swollen grotesquely. There are sutures all over, tubes and a strong smell of hospital. When I look at John, I see the anguish in his face.

❦

The first week I am not aware of anything but discomfort. There seems no place to put my swollen head, and my mind keeps carrying me back to where I don't want to go. The anaesthetic and the painkillers sedate me heavily. I feel alone, though the nurses are in and out all the time, monitoring vital signs, checking grafts, doing suture care, administering medications. My left shoulder and hip hurt; so do my head and my stomach. *I* hurt. I can't stay conscious. Trevor is being cared for next door, they tell me. Sometimes someone is holding my hand. Still, I feel so alone. I am blinded, my eyelids cut and swollen shut. Blackness is all around me and within.

I hear quiet crying. Someone's face is close to mine. Soft breathing. A whisper.

"I love you, Patricia. I love you both so much."

I want to smile. I want to speak. I can't. My mind floats. Bonnie. Trevor's sister. What is she doing here? Soothing words. I love you. Cradled in darkness, I fall down, down, down and away.

🐚

Jane Durnie (younger sister)

I am twenty years old, the last of the ten of us living at home. I sleep late that Sunday morning. My Auntie Gerry, who is visiting us, comes down the hallway to my room. She startles me awake with cold hands on my face. "Jane Ellen? There's been an accident."

The words do not sink in at first. I dress, then speak with my father on the phone when he calls from the hospital. He asks me to give Auntie Gerry a scotch. Never having done this before, I pour her half a glass. The doorbell rings. Two huge policemen are there, asking for my mother and father. When I tell them my parents are already at the hospital, the policemen seem relieved. One of them lets out all his breath at once.

"I can only offer you our extreme sympathy," he says. They turn back down the steps.

I call out to their retreating backs. "Wait. Where did the accident happen? Was the car totalled?" The men look at me in surprise.

"I'm sorry," says the taller one, "I thought you knew. It was a bear attack."

Fear is the biggest feeling. No one knows what to expect.

I am relieved when I first see Trish, because she is still herself. She is profoundly swollen, with many, many stitches, but she is still Patricia, and she will live.

❦

The nurse speaks to me. Way above the steep black pit my bed lies in is her tiny head. They need an X-ray of my jaw, she says. They might have to wire it shut. Her voice is joined by several others. More tiny heads become hot-pink pixies dancing at the edge of the blackness.

I move my arms to check my position. I am lying crooked on the bed. I hear my mother's voice. When did she come? Oh, Mom, I wish you didn't have to know about this. They want to move me. Please don't make me move. Please. But I *am* being moved, onto a stretcher. I hear whimpering, then realize it's me.

Hands surround my head, placing a flat pillow under it. I'm propped on my right side. So tired. So sore. The stretcher moves, and I sense the brighter light of the hall. It hurts my eyes, although they are swollen shut. I hear whispering. We stop. Footsteps walk away, then return. A cloth is being placed on my head, very lightly. The stretcher moves again.

"What are you doing?" It hurts to talk. There's no answer. "What is the cloth for?" I know there's somebody there. It's hard to breathe under here.

"It's to cover your head."

To cover my head? Why?

"Take it off. Too stuffy."

They don't want people to see me. They are hiding my head. Oh God.

The cloth is removed. I try smiling at the voices. I can't see the staring anyway. My mind drifts away. What's wrong with my head?

The stretcher lurches in and out of the elevator. With each lurch, I hear someone cry out. The voices around me are gentle, patient. But I am afraid. They want me to sit, to stand up, to walk. The world whirls crazily. The X-ray has to be done with me sitting down, the voices explain. My head is enormous, and my neck can't hold it up. The voices talk softly, telling me the machine will rotate around me, will make noise. Hold still.

I hear something loud. I feel the machine brush my forehead, and I cringe. Please, don't hit my head. I'm in a panic, huddled and alone. One more time, the voices say. They fuzz over. I'm going to fall. To slip. No! How do I get out of here? I want to go back to bed. Please. Help me.

"Just one more picture," the X-ray voice says cheerfully. My nurse's voice says no for me. No more X-rays today. I feel myself lifted onto the stretcher. The voices dull and disappear. The stretcher cuts through the black. I float.

My family is with me. There is always someone when I call out. My brothers come, six big men. I feel the large roughness of their hands gently touching mine. They take turns squatting beside the bed, faces close to my pain, their voices uncertain. "I love you." "Hang in there, Trish." "I'm praying for you." Soft, whispered comfort wafting through the agony that is my enormous head, allowing me to drift and rest a moment.

❧

Bernie Van Tighem (younger brother)

I get the call in Foremost, Alberta, where I work for a geophysical exploration company. It has been a short day, and it's still light when I am summoned to the manager's office. The message is "Phone home immediately," with no reason given.

I think of many things while walking across the motel parking lot to the outside payphone. It can't be anything, though. Nothing bad ever happens to us, just to other people.

I am baffled when my parents' part-time housekeeper answers the phone. She is noncommittal at first, saying only that none of my brothers are there to talk to me. I am confused. I can't imagine why she is answering the phone, nor why any of my brothers would be at home. None of them live there any more.

They are all at the hospital, she suddenly bursts out. I press her for a reason. As she responds, my throat closes up and my eyes fill with tears. "Your brother and sister were savagely mutilated by a grizzly bear," she says. "Come home as fast as you can."

The blood rushes past my ears, sounding like a train. I press for more information. Who was it who was injured? But all she knows is that someone was attacked while hiking in Waterton and is now in serious condition at the Foothills Hospital.

"Come home as fast as you can."

I pack, and the company arranges for bus tickets to Calgary. Waiting for a connector in Medicine Hat, I decide this is taking too long. I find the nearest car-rental firm.

The trip to Calgary is not the safest I have ever made. A few times I pull over to phone for updates, and only as I enter Calgary do I learn it is Trevor and Patricia who have been hurt.

I drive straight to Foothills. I try to get information at the reception desk about Trevor and Patricia's whereabouts, with no success. The receptionist will not even confirm that they are at this hospital. Luckily, my sister Jane and her husband, Greg, have already made it inside, and they arrive to get me past the gauntlet. I find out later that several newspaper reporters have attempted to sneak in for photographs and interviews.

Upstairs there is confusion and anger as a reporter is escorted out of the intensive care ward. I look into Trevor's room. His dim shape lies still, and his family is crowded around the bed. I join my family next to Patricia's bandaged form.

Back at my parents' house, my brothers Tom and Greg and I decide we'll go to pick up Patricia and Trevor's stuff from Waterton. There is no urgency for the trip, but we need something to do. Waiting at the hospital is excruciating.

By the time we arrive in Waterton, they have located and killed the bear responsible. The warden offers to let us see her. Being in the presence of the bear that has wreaked such damage on my family is chilling. I don't know if it makes me feel any better, though, seeing her dead. She was just an animal doing what animals do.

The next time I see Patricia, she is awake and coherent. I am at a loss for words, not knowing how to talk to someone so messed up. My mom has cautioned us not to dwell on Patricia's appearance, because she is concerned about it. When she rolls over in bed, I get my first good look at the part of her face not covered by bandages. I am struck by her resemblance to me. With the swelling caused by her injuries, her face is broad and round like mine.

"Now I see why people say we look alike." Too late, I realize I should have said nothing. Patricia wants to know what I mean, asking over and over, "Why? What's the matter with my face? What do I look like? What's wrong?"

It takes Mom some time to calm her down.

I am Queen Tut. I sit high above the world in a glass-walled room. My sister Jane and my mother are visiting. I can't see them, but I know they are there. My mother tells me I have received more flowers, and my mind paints an enormous bouquet of vibrant colours. I laugh, sitting regally high on my soft eiderdown bed. I like flowers. I have so many. My glass room is filled from top to bottom. Behind them are bright striped curtains, shielding me from the other glass rooms up and down the hospital corridor.

The resident will be in soon to start my IV, someone says. They tell me his name. Ha! I know all about him. No way. No IV. Not on me. I am the queen. I don't want another poke. My hands are so sore already.

He's here. I gaze down at him from my bed, his white lab coat in sharp contrast to all my flowers. He is very small. His voice is kind, reassuring. But I won't let him win me over. He's explaining why I have to have an IV, telling me where he will place it. No. His hands are warm and gentle. No! I don't want the IV there. Put it in up higher, I tell him. I know my spot is better. But he doesn't listen. The needle pokes and stings. He's missed the vein.

"Sorry."

I want to scream and punch and cry. Queen Tut begins to

shrivel. The resident tries again, and this time he's got it. But I don't want the IV there. It hurts. I can't bend my wrist. And how can I reach my suction now?

Sadness smashes down on my head. I'm in the hospital. I was mauled by a bear, and Trevor, lying next door, was mauled too. I hurt everywhere.

Queen Tut is gone. I'm just me, Patricia, wrapped in black. The bright flowers, glass walls and striped curtains are gone. If there are flowers in my room, I can't see them. My mother tells me there are. I want so badly to see. To know where I am. To orient myself. To challenge the recurring images of the bear coming at me in the tree. The resident is gone. The IV fluid pours into my vein, and I grope with my free hand for the flow control, cursing residents who always leave IVs wide open.

❧

The room is hot. The nurses have finished my evening suture care, placing antibiotic ointment along the length of every suture line: across my scalp, over and over; across my nose and forehead and cheek; under my chin. I hate it. They are gone now, and I am alone, swollen and hurting.

But there are hands on my head. I hit at the air. Go away! Leave me alone! But no one is there. My hands cut through the space above my head. I'm frightened.

"Hello?"

No answer. I'm sure I heard someone come in, but no one answers.

The hands are there again. I hit at them. Nothing but air. Panic.

"Who's there?"

No answer. I curl up, back to the side rail. Don't touch me! I pull the covers up to my chin. Everything's black. I want to tear my face off, find my old one beneath so that I can see again.

"Hello?" Tentatively this time. Still no answer. Am I going crazy? Those hands, picking at and rubbing my head. They aren't really there. Be calm, Patricia. It's just sensations. I cower in my bed.

Something *is* in my room, even if I can't see it. Somebody help me! It must be the middle of the night. Frantically, I fight with the bed covers to find my call bell. There are hands all over me.

Almost immediately, there's a voice. A kind, female voice. A nurse. Eagerly, I turn my head towards her.

Oh God!

It is black all around my pit. The kind voice is a giant bat, hairy, black and brown. It hovers above me, wings open wide. Huge, shiny, black eyes. I feel myself shrink down into the bed. Whimpering.

"What's the matter?" the voice wants to know. "Do you need something? "

I can't talk. I feel mouth-dry horror. It's coming down on me, coming down into my pit. It's the length of my bed. What can I do? Shrivel into a ball. Away from that thing.

The voice is gone. The bat, too. I hear voices outside my room, in the hallway, then footsteps. I'm scared to raise my head. But I do. Help me.

I want to scream. There are two bats now, one on each side of my bed, hovering above me. Expressionless, huge, hairy faces. Teeth. Black. The voices are sympathetic, soft. A small, warm hand cradles mine.

"What's the matter? Can you tell me?"

I want to disappear into the security of that voice. I try to talk, but I'm crying. The bats hover above me, staring. Enormous, quivering bodies.

I'm burning up. There's sudden confusion. The room is full of voices, up and down. My brother Gordon. My mother. The resident. He's changing the analgesic order, he says.

The room is filled with wide wings and faces with pointy sharp teeth. Mom is real, I know. The bats aren't. I hear Mom's voice. I like it. I know that voice so well. Her small hands hold mine. I feel her wedding ring. The bats are there, but they are less threatening now.

The nurse is back with a needle. I don't want it. I'm agitated. Fearful. Hot. Yes, I hurt. Okay, if it won't make me wacky. If you're sure. I want to relax, leave the world behind.

Mom is here. And a pill, too. What is it? Never mind. I'll take it. And a fan. That's nice. Blow the heat away. Hold on to me, Mom, I don't know where I'm going. It's only early evening. I wish it were morning. I wish it were next month. Or last month.

The drugs carry me away. The bats are gone. I am just me again in my bed. Just me, sore and swollen and unable to see. It's black around and inside me. Quiet night, calm, cooler. Sleep.

✿

Kevin Van Tighem (older brother)

W *hen the phone rang, I jumped up and blundered into the kitchen in the dark. If it wasn't a wrong number, it had to be bad news, I thought.*

At first, I didn't even know who it was. A man's voice, deep and choking, like he was drunk or something. Then I realized it was my father. He was trying to get words out past deep emotion. My heart almost seized up on me. Had something happened to my mother? I had never heard my father sound anything like that, and it shook me deeply. I tried to get him to talk normally.

"Something's happened," he said finally. There was a pause, then he started again. "There's been an accident. Your sister . . ."

I wondered which sister. I had an image of a car accident.

"There's been a bear attack," he said, his voice stronger this time. "Patricia and Trevor are hurt. I'm at the Foothills Hospital."

There was a kind of relief at least in knowing who and what. Now I could begin to wrap my mind around it. I asked Dad if I should come to Calgary. He said to wait until morning, as they were still in surgery. The injuries didn't appear to be life-threatening. I said something clumsy and inadequate about taking care of himself. I was frustrated when I hung up that I had failed so miserably at showing my feelings for him or for Patricia. It was one of those moments when I realize how much I withdraw emotionally when the people I love most are hurt or in need.

Lying awake in bed, I snuggled up to my wife's back, resting my hand on her pregnant belly in the darkness. I wondered if I should get into the car and drive to Calgary right away. I wished I had asked more questions. I tried to imagine how the attack could have happened.

Gail and I were so caught up in our own adventure just then — our first home, a baby on the way, my new job. I had just finished my last year of working on park wildlife inventories. I had been based in Glacier National Park, a part of British Columbia noted for grizzlies and black bears, dense vegetation and rugged terrain. I had started exploring the high country a decade earlier with an almost blasé attitude towards bears, but this past summer in Glacier had worn me down with one encounter after another.

In June, I had blundered into a large, dominant black bear in dense young aspen forest. The bear refused to retreat and, when I shouted loudly, lowered its head and laid back its ears, glaring at me. Legs rubbery, I was the one to retreat. Later that month, I encountered three *grizzly bears in as many days, including one that sneaked within twenty yards to investigate the noises I was making. It was as startled as I was once we saw each other. I went up a tree, and the bear fled.*

By the end of the field season, my nerves were badly frayed. In August, I had one habitat type left to sample for small mammals, an alder-choked avalanche path. Standing at the edge of the Trans-Canada Highway with a bag of peanut-butter–smeared Museum Special traps in a bag on my shoulder, I looked down into the green jungle and told myself that Parks Canada would just have to live without knowing what rodents ruled its tangles. I couldn't bring myself to face the near certainty of close-range bear encounters in such prime habitat. I went home, feeling off balance and wondering why my long fascination with bears was being overpowered by a sense of vulnerability.

The morning after getting Dad's call, Gail and I drove to Calgary. At my parents' house, Mom was tightlipped and strong, controlling her emotions in order to keep functioning. Soon Greg arrived. He is big and burly, with one of the biggest hearts of anyone I know. He walked in, went straight to Mom and folded her in a hug. She broke down and wept.

At the hospital, several people were waiting in Patricia's ward: Dad, our Auntie Gerry, my sister Margaret, and other siblings. Gail had to leave right away; the medicated stuffiness of the room reacted with her pregnancy to turn her stomach. Patricia spoke to us, and Gail said later that if it hadn't been for the voice, she would never have recognized the person in the bed.

I was shocked to my core at the sight of Patricia. I couldn't see specific injuries, but her face was swollen up like a soccer ball. She was groggy from drugs but was still able to answer questions. I didn't stay long. I didn't know what to say.

❧

What holds me together? I don't know. I am a bundle of soreness and stiffness, a beaten person. I swim in the blackness as someone helps me up. Fatigue hits me like a wind. Hands have a firm grasp on my arms. They are moving me to a chair, getting me off the sore right side that I've lain on for almost two weeks. Somewhere inside *I* am. This body encases me, but I am not it.

I listen with amazement to the mournful sounds coming from my mouth. Encouraging female voices blanket me. The chair is upholstered, they say. It will just be for a minute, while they change the bed and put a special mattress on it. My right side won't hurt so much then. I want to get up. I want to get moving. I want to get better. The inside me encourages but is amazed at the effort, the fatigue, the pain of the body.

Ease into the chair. Mouth dry, mind dull. Breathing fast. Head bulbous on frail neck sways.

I mumble words through thick lips. "Can I see Trevor?" There's a soft noise nearby, a hand on my arm.

"What was that, Trish? What did you say?"

"Can I visit Trevor? I want to."

My outside aches and stings with sitting. But sitting is half-way there. Maybe I could get up to be with him. I feel my mind and body beginning to come together, awakening to place and person and want. Gripping the arms of the chair, I speak to the kind voice beside me.

"Please? In a wheelchair. Just to say hi." Somewhere behind the pain and the blackness is enormous yearning.

"I'll run and get one."

Somewhere at the back of everything, in a small voice muffled by confusion, is a faint cry.

Trevor. I want my Trevor.

❦

He was across the room from me at the party. Sitting close beside him, laughing up at him, was a blonde. A blown-dry, stylishly dressed and beautiful blonde. They had arrived together. He'd said hello to me and then gone to get her a plate of food. I'd come to this party because I knew he'd be here. I was drawn to his tall stature and calm mannerisms and precise, direct speech. Who was the blonde? I'd heard he had just broken up with his girlfriend. Did he have another one already? Why did he keep looking at me? Almost as though he were flirting?

A yellow balloon drifted across talking heads into my lap. A dark-bearded face peered around the bodies and motioned me to hit the balloon back. A pink balloon came across, and then a green one. Amid the chatter and heat of party bodies, we rallied balloons and grinned foolishly at each other. We finally met on the stairs, face to face. People were pushing past us to get to the washroom.

"Hi." Suddenly we were shy. Trevor was talking. He told me his family was at the party, too. The blonde was his fourteen-year-old sister. I laughed. Come, he invited me, and I'll introduce you. Did I like this party? No, I said, and yes. I laughed again. How could I tell him that I only came because I knew he would be there? Would I like to go somewhere else? Yes. Let's go somewhere else.

We left the party and drifted out into the cool fall night. We pooled the dollar-fifty we had between us to get a Cinzano at a nearby lounge, then sat in his rebuilt old sports car in front of my parents' house, talking. Not even a kiss at the end, but a promise of see you later, and a mutual delirious glow. I floated into the house.

❧

Someone's pushing my wheelchair out the door. There's a flash of light. I duck my head, hold tight to the chair arms. Stay up, I tell myself. We go around a corner and into dimness again. I hear Trevor's father, Daun. Trevor's just gone to sleep, he says. Let's put Trish here. No, not there, over here. There's talking, scraping, bumping. The noise and confusion and move-ment of unseen bodies send my head into loops of crazy pain. I want to be alone with Trevor. Why can't everyone shut up and leave us alone?

The room smells like sickness. I feel the hospital bed in front of me, my knees touching linen and a cold metal edge. I hear snuffly, thick breathing. My head is heavy.

"Trevor?"

I hear myself speak. Spin, spin, spin. Darkness all around. I reach and fumble through the bed rails.

"Trevor?" Louder this time.

The breathing continues, thick and noisy. He's working to breathe. My searching hand finds a body, a leg, under the bed covers. I follow the shape. Find a hand. Limp, big hand. Trevor. Warm and solid.

"Hi, Trevor." I grasp his hand, willing it to close around mine. The voices in the room are gone. Everything's hushed. I'm screaming inside my head. Trevor! Please!

One big finger makes a slow-motion caress on the back of my hand. "Uh mish." Hi, Trish. I want to throw his hand from me. To kick the bed. Talk to me! Be okay!

I'm aching. Hurting. Trapped in the dark with this strange breathing and a dead hand. Get me out of here. Now.

"He just had a shot, Trish. He's quite sedated."

But I am no longer here. Inside, I sob, fighting the tangle of

47

confusion. On the outside, I sit quietly, tuck Trevor's hand under the covers, grip my chair handles, tilt my face down towards my lap.

From dim to bright to dim again. The wheelchair's rubber wheels are almost soundless on the hospital floor. I'm lifted back into bed. Clean, new sheets and a softer mattress. Pillows propped against my back and head and legs cradle me. I lie still and unmoving when the long needle is poked into my left buttock, and I wait for the drugs to take me away.

✺

I know Dr. Potter from the general surgery floor where I used to work. He was a resident there and now he's a resident here, doing a plastic surgery rotation. He was on call with our surgeon the day of the accident. I can't see him, but I recognize his voice. I've told him already that he knows me too. I reminded him of the day he and I stood in the hall as I was going off shift and talked about residencies in New Zealand. My husband was a medical student, I'd said, and we were looking into the possibility of living in another country for a while. But though Dr. Potter says he remembers talking that day, he doesn't remember me. I *want* him to remember. I *know* he knows me.

He has come into my room now. It's daytime. I can sense that from the hospital sounds around me. There are other people with him. I can hear the shuffling of their feet on the floor.

"Hi." I speak to the right of my bed, where I know the group is standing.

"You had a pretty bad night last night," Dr. Potter says. That's true. It was a horrible night. Nightmares and hallucinations.

I tell him how much I wish I could see. Even just for a minute, to orient myself. My right eyelids are cut and swollen shut, and I've been told my left eye is covered with grafts of muscle and skin taken from other parts of my body. He listens, says I could try to open my right eye with my fingers. I feel a surge of happiness.

My fingers are tentative, exploring. Where's the opening, anyway? It doesn't feel like an eye up there. Puffy. Crusty. Yuck. I pry it open. Ouch. Gently. A crack. There! Light and Dr. Potter's legs. I try to shift my head, desperate to see a face. He's bending over me.

Friendly big grin. Red beard and hair. Yep, that's him. He's beaming, and so am I. Lots of other peering, bending faces behind him. Other smiles.

"Can you see?"

"Yes!"

From my tiny peephole, I can see that I'm in a private room. I've been in rooms like this so many times taking care of patients. It's just a plain old hospital room. Not a pit. No bats or pixies. Just the hospital, and smiling faces all around.

My eye is sore. I let it shut and breathe deeply. I feel peace, but

I have to open my eye again. With my fingers. Ouch. Wonderful. Colour and light and people and faces. How fantastic to see how normal everything is. To see.

❦

The deep voice that speaks is my father's. With it comes an image of Dad in brown pants, his favourite blue cardigan, brown leather shoes with a design of little dots on top. He always wore that kind of shoe. An old pair for fishing trips to wear under tall hip waders while piggybacking us kids across a stream. A newer pair that a small daughter would stand on, her arms around his waist, walking with him from the car to the house when he came home from the office. Another pair for Saturday work in the garden and drives to and from ballet lessons and the library. The stern step of those shoes down the long hallway in our house would send our small bodies hurtling back to our own beds after lights out, pushing our faces against pillows to stifle giggles and closing our eyes in a concentrated attempt to look asleep. The tall and solid image of him is comforting to that small daughter within me. His chair is pulled close to the bed, and one long arm stretches over me. His big hand encompasses mine. The dreams can't get hold of me now.

Is it night or day? Dad tells me it's the middle of the night, and he will stay with me till morning. He reads to me from a book about American heroes he found in the solarium. I listen to stories of Paul Revere and Florence Nightingale. The words mean little to me, but they are a diversion.

The hospital world is still. The hum of the fan and Dad's voice lull me. I feel calm, knowing Trevor is next door. According to my nurse's last report, Trevor's mother sat knitting beside his bed until he slept. I want to sleep too. Dad's deep voice reads on. His big, warm hand holds mine. I start to drift. The last painkiller is working. I feel fuzzy, exhausted, halfway asleep and sinking.

It's in the hall again. It's headed for my room. My heart sinks. My mouth dries up. No! Where can I go? How did it get here? A ridiculous picture of the bear in the elevator, pushing "3" for the third floor, torments me. Or up the stairs? It knows where to go, where to find me. I have to move fast. I feel paralyzed. To the bathroom. Quick. Lock myself in. It's here. Breathing and snorting and woofing on the other side of the door. I hear its long claws scratching. My heart is going to jump out of my body. Go away. Go away. It's butting at the door. It's going to get in. What can I do now? Go away!

"Patricia!"

The voice comes sharply. I fight to wake. Struggle to know where I am. Someone has a viselike grip on my hands. It hurts, but I'm squeezing back frantically. Breathing fast. Heart loud. The bear must still be here somewhere. Dry mouth. Lick my lips.

"Patricia. Wake up."

It's Dad. I can feel my body soften. I'm in the hospital. There are no bears here. I wish I could be sure of that.

I loosen one hand from Dad's grasp and reach up. Pry my mucky right eye open.

The room is dim. A triangle of yellow light from the hallway falls across my bed. The shadowy figure of my father is leaning over me, his face in darkness. There are no bears behind him. There are no bears at the bathroom door. I sigh and let my eye shut again. I'm so tired. Dad talks to me. I listen to the calming, low murmur of his voice and relax, breathing deeply.

"You still have your beautiful mouth, you know." His voice is close, almost a whisper. Did he really say that? I feel a flush of pleasure and surprise wash over me, and smile in response, too tired to speak. With my hands softly pocketed in his, I listen to the fan hum and shyly savour his words. The hospital is quiet around me. Trevor is next door. We're okay. I sleep.

❦

Margaret Bailey (older sister)

I took the Greyhound from Edmonton to Calgary, and my brothers Tom and Greg met me at the station in a big rental truck. They were serious and grim-faced and furious at what the media had been doing, trying to get pictures of Trish and Trevor in emergency and ICU and pestering Trevor's mom, Sarah, who had been staying in their home.

My brother Bernard had told me Patricia looked mongoloid. His description was callous but accurate, and it helped me when I first saw her. She was so swollen that there was no place to touch her or hug her. She couldn't hear me crying or saying I loved her. I pulled a chair up beside the bed and found a finger — the ring finger on her left hand looked okay. I sat beside her and very gently stroked the finger and talked to her. I was so scared. She wasn't here, really, and I was afraid she would never come back.

Later, I tried to help her take ice or hold a straw to drink, and she swatted my hand away. She was blind and barely conscious, but she had to do it herself. She could identify staff and visitors by touch, smell and voice. Still only slightly conscious, she had insisted on a sign over her bed saying, "My name is not Pat. Please call me Patricia or Trish."

Weeks later, I helped her out of the bath. She was 110 pounds with a huge, swollen head and so much dignity. She was too weak to bathe herself, but she would not allow pity.

Sitting by the window in her hospital room, I watched the golden, glorious fall unfold along the river outside. I became aware of a man who kept appearing at the door that stood open, looking at Patricia. She was in and out of sleep, bandaged and totally defenceless. The more often I saw him, the more upset I became. Finally I told the nurses, who were protective of Patricia, and he never came back. He was an orderly from another unit, they said, curious about her injuries and the attack.

❧

I miss *Trevor*, not this guy standing in the doorway of my room, asking if he can come in. I lie in bed on my right side, my "good" side, and stare at him. He's been in to visit a few times, but I can't get used to the way he looks. His face balloons out on one side and is zigzagged with red lines and black sutures. His nose is swollen, crooked and distorted. His jaw is wired shut, and he can't move his lips. He has to hold them open with his fingers when he talks. His speech is slurred. He can't seem to catch his breath, and his breathing is laboured and loud.

I feel so angry I want to turn away. But I can't. It hurts too much to move, and there's no other way I can lie. I want to tell him to get lost, standing there so hesitant and skinny. I don't want to look at him or listen to him breathe, yet I also yearn to hold him close and cry. Seeing him brings a tangle of emotions to the back of my throat, and I want to throw up. I can't tell him to leave. I can't tell him that seeing him makes me feel sick and angry and sad.

He stares back at my good eye from his twisted face, questioning. He continues into the room and sits in the chair at my back, his noisy, strained breathing the only sound. "Trish?" I feel myself stiffen even before his hand comes to rest on my shoulder.

I can't see him behind me, but my mind is full of his contorted face and the dark sadness in his left eye. The other eye shows no expression. That side of his face doesn't move anymore.

I'm hot. Irritable. I hurt. I want that warm hand to feel good, but it doesn't. I am restless, so tired of this game. I would love to hit something. My hands are too sore, though. Anger wells.

He wants to know how I feel. His voice is soft. He squeezes my shoulder gently. Go away. Go away. I love you. Soundlessly. I am crying inside. "Ah Trevor, what happened? What happened?" I want to scream it.

I hear him get up and move around the bed. I shut my eye against the sight of his half-shaved head. I can't understand my feelings. The minute he goes, I'll wish he were here again. He crouches beside my bed, and I open my eye to gaze dully at him. He rests his forehead on the side rails and lets one hand come between the metal bars to touch mine. Anger surges again within me. I shut my eye. I am exhausted. Emotions spin crazily in my head.

"I love you, my Trish." Trevor's voice comes out of the twisted face in front of me. I wince. He pauses to breathe, then the slurred quiet words come again, telling me that he is tired and will see me later. We both smile, small smiles. He's gone.

"Trevor?"

I see his thin legs, below loose, short pyjama bottoms, moving out the door.

❧

It's morning again. I lie still in my bed, on my right side, reluctant to begin another day. The view is boring. At eye level are the brown drawers and closet where my belongings are kept. I have to move very cautiously to see anything else in the room. There is someone at my door. Slowly I turn, supporting my heavy head so I can sit up. Ouch.

It's Dr. Potter. Good. I like to visit with him. I can show him my sore IV site and ask if he'd be willing to try to find another vein somewhere. I know I'm rumpled and stained and mucky, nothing too sweet to look at, but I smile crookedly at him. "Good morning."

He looks puzzled as he comes slowly to the end of my bed. He bends slightly and peers through his glasses. His eyes widen in surprise. "I do know you!"

I feel my smile widen. Of course you do. I told you you did.

"I remember you now." Straightening up, he laughs quietly, shaking his head, his eyes still fixed on me.

I am happy. I feel a release. Some Patricia is back in my face.

❦

My room is green. It's a pale green, pockmarked with chips out of the plaster. It's due for painting soon, so we are allowed to tape cards on the wall. My mother and sisters do that, and the wall at the end of my bed is colourful with good wishes. Trevor's room is decorated the same way.

We've been here almost three weeks. I can see now. I can even open my right eye without using my fingers. But my eye tires fast and doesn't like the light. My curtains are always drawn, and my brother Tom says my room is depressing. I don't care. All I want to do is rest and sleep and stop thinking.

Someone is at the door.

I don't want to visit. I don't feel like talking right now. I close my eye.

It sounds like my mother, moving around the room. She places something in my locker, then moves around to sit in the chair at my back. Her voice comes quietly.

"There are some Mass cards here for you, along with your other cards." She pauses. "The phone has been ringing constantly with messages from people praying for you. I've written them down. You can see them later."

Praying for me? What good is that? If I collect enough prayers do I get my face back? I keep my eye shut, feigning sleep. Mom falls silent. As I drift in and out, her words play through my mind, comforting me this time. Cards, phone calls, prayers: people care about me. I float and relax.

Is Mom gone? How long has it been? There's no sound, and I call her quietly. "Mom?"

Immediately there's a light touch on my shoulder.

"I'm hurting again."

"Do you need a shot? I can get a nurse for you." The shots make me so sleepy. Then I can't visit when I do feel like it. But I hurt.

"Maybe see if there's someone around. I think I do want one. Yes."

The shots are friendly. A shot will send me away for a while, to uninterrupted dozing not coloured with pictures of Trevor's face and the other pictures that rise in my mind. The pictures that bring nausea and fear: the bear's face on mine, the bear pacing and staring with small black eyes.

Mom is back with a nurse. She brings the chair around to my front, where I can see her. I ask her to hold my hand till the shot starts to work. Her face is familiar and comforting but tense. Her mouth curves upward in a tiny smile.

"Go to sleep if you can. I'll sit here."

"You look tired, Mom." The words come slowly. I can feel the effects of the needle.

Her hand squeezes mine. Her eyes are closed, her head back on the tall chair. Her forehead is furrowed. I want to reach out and rub it like I used to. I remember perching on the arm of a chair beside her, my skinny child body ready for bed in a favourite soft pink nightie. Mom's stockinged feet would be propped on the footstool, her hands idle in her lap. She'd rest her head on the back of the chair, eyes closed, as the sounds of my brothers and sisters swirled around us. Against a background of records playing, arguments over who would get the bathtub next, loud card games, and frustration with math homework, my small fingers would massage her brow. I'd watch carefully as her face relaxed. Groggy now from the painkiller, I am angry that this accident had to happen and interfere with her life. It doesn't seem fair. Once again I wish fervently that somehow I could have kept this from her.

"Mom?" I speak quietly. "Do you remember how busy it was when we were little? I always wanted more of you."

She nods. "You would cry after I'd tucked you in. I'd come back to your bedroom and sit beside you, rubbing your back."

"I always wanted you to stay longer. I wanted to feel like an only child. Remember going for a doctor's appointment? We'd ride the bus there and back. That was the best, because I got to spend a few hours alone with you."

Mom's face softens as she laughs. "The refreshment counter at Woolworth's. I would take you for a treat afterward, and we'd sit on those pivoting stools."

"You had a bran muffin. Always." I smile at her. "And I would have Jell-O, in little bright-green squares. Like they try to get me to eat in here."

Her features have relaxed some. I let my eye close and float with the medication, our hands firmly linked on top of the cover.

❧

For an instant, I'm unsure if I am dead or just dreaming. Very faintly, there is music. Singing and voices harmonizing, rising and falling. I laugh aloud, wondering if it is celestial. It feels good to laugh. Mom, sitting at my bedside, hears it too. It's coming from somewhere down the hall. Someone must be listening to a radio or a tape. I want to find it. I want to hear it better.

I propose a walk. It's been a week since my last surgery, and for the first time since the accident, I feel a surge of energy. Mom helps me to stand up. I wait for a moment, until my head stops spinning, then Mom helps me into slippers and drapes my blue terrycloth housecoat, a present from the medical students in Trevor's class, over my shoulders. As she has seen the nurses do, she carefully positions a clean white towel to catch the drips from the soft rubber drains protruding from my shorn, sutured scalp.

On my way out the door, I shoot a fast look at the mirror above the sink. I do this every time I pass, catching quick glimpses of a tall, thin form, a big head. Today, my glance shows someone with hunched shoulders and spots of yellow drainage on a white towel.

The lights are dimmed up and down the hallway. It's evening, peaceful. Doors to patients' rooms are open, and there is the sound of occasional laughter and low voices. At the far end of the hall, a nurse comes out of one room and goes into another.

We walk towards the patient recreation room. The singing is coming from there. We trundle along slowly, my one arm holding on to Mom and the other pushing my IV pole noisily beside me. Its little wheels squeak intermittently, and the small white unicorn clip my sister Jane has brought me swings from the tubing.

Once we're out of the unit hallway, the lights are bright and hard on my good eye. My eye waters, blurring my vision, and I let go of Mom's arm frequently to wipe it with a tissue. The tear duct for that eye is gone. It's one of the things that can perhaps be fixed later. Until then, it requires constant mopping. Trevor wasn't in his room as we went by, and I'm disappointed. I would have liked to have him along on this little adventure. I would like him to see me up walking and feeling happy.

They are singing hymns. No wonder it sounds like heaven. It is a Mennonite choir: men and women and little ones in black and plaids and kerchiefs and aprons, clustered at one end of the large room, their heads held high. Their faces are round and rosy-cheeked. Voices mingle, high and low, young and old, rising and falling. I'd love to sit and listen all evening. A woman beckons us to come in, but I shake my head. I wouldn't last five minutes. There are too many people in the rec room, and the choir is over-whelmingly loud. I'm tired already. It's time to head back. I've found the source of the music and am pleased with that.

This is the longest walk I've taken since I got here, Mom points out, congratulating me. A man and a woman leaving the unit stare. I ignore them, feeling proud of myself. Nurses return-ing from coffee break whiz by us, smiling over their shoulders and telling me how well I'm doing. Will I ever walk that fast again? Wear a uniform? I wonder what I look like to them. I'm a nurse too.

A group of people has entered my room. It's too much to open my eye and be surrounded by the faces and white lab coats of morning rounds. I try to boost myself up a little higher in the bed, straightening my gown and yellow bed covers. The curtains are drawn. The room is dim and smells of antiseptic. After another night of tossing and turning, it was good to sleep in. I am more rested now, but I feel disgusting. I haven't been up yet to wash. I wish I had at least washed my face. My head drains have leaked through onto my neck and shoulders, and I can feel crusting around my right eye. My suture lines are smeared with antibiotic ointment, and some has rubbed off onto my pillow. Part of my liquid breakfast sits on the front of my gown; my sore mouth won't work properly.

Dianne, the head nurse, moves to open the curtains, and a flood of bright autumn light hits the room. I squint and cringe away from all the eyes on me. I wish I had changed into one of the flowered, tie-at-the-back gowns my sister brought me.

Dr. Lewis is the plastic surgeon who put Trevor and me back together. His face is friendly. Young. His eyes are kind, his smile small and hesitant. He never says much. When he does speak, he has a slight Scottish accent. I have only heard him laugh once, when I asked him if my nose had been broken. Then he threw his head back and almost giggled. "In about a million pieces," he said.

Today, he appears preoccupied, his face solemn as he sits on the edge of my bed. His hands are firm, examining my scalp, instructing Dianne which sutures can come out. I feel myself tense. My head is so tender and so ugly. I would like to pull it away and hide under the covers. I would like to disappear.

He wants to examine my face now, and my eyes. Dianne stands close beside the doctor listening to his instructions. She makes eye contact with me and grins. I smile back. We're friends. She is small and moves quickly. Her hand rests on my leg as Dr. Lewis asks me to look from side to side. I move my hand near Dianne's. She holds it, and I feel calmer.

Behind Dianne are the residents and someone I know must be a third-year medical student. Directly in front of me is Dr. Milton, tall and good-looking with a dark moustache and eyes. He is the brother of a friend of mine, a nurse I went to school with. I knew he was a plastic surgery resident, though I wasn't sure what "plastics" meant then. Well, I am now: repairs and minuscule sutures. When I met him last year in a café, I could never have anticipated that this would be the next place I'd see him, towering above my bed in his blue operating-room garb and lab jacket.

"How's it going?" His tone is gentle. I don't answer, only smile wanly. I feel miserable, and the smell of antiseptic is sickening.

Another resident glances occasionally at a bunch of papers in his hands, appearing restless. Then, with a whispered something to Dr. Milton and one hasty look in my direction, he leaves the room. I am happy to see the medical student leave with him. I didn't even look to see who the student was. He must be a classmate of Trevor's, and I thought he might avoid my glance. I feel less self-conscious without so many people gathered around my bed.

Dr. Lewis addresses me now, direct and calm. I reach for his hand, feeling a need for the warm touch, and I am pleased when it accepts mine. How am I sleeping? he asks. How am I eating? How does my eye feel? He waits for my answers, smiling at my attempts at humour. He informs me of plans for another surgery this week. He will remove the dead scalp at the back of my head and do some revisions of my left-eye area. Do I have any questions?

There is a long pause. I can't answer. I feel sore and tired and confused. I can't register what he has told me, and I can't form any intelligent questions. I need to have everyone go away so that I can think. Shrugging, I tell him, "I'm just tired."

The visit is over. I smile. I want the smile to tell them all how much I appreciate their contact and caring and gentleness, but I don't trust my messy face. I don't know it any more. It doesn't smile like it used to, and I don't know what message it sends.

They are gone. The room is quiet. I close my eye and collapse back on the pillow, letting the room spin emptily around me.

A voice at my door calls, "Patricia?"

Looking up, I see Dianne's face poking around the corner.

"I'll take those sutures out for you. I'll be there in a minute."

The face disappears. I feel glad. Dianne is experienced and kind, and she wants me to have as little discomfort as possible. Emotion washes over me, and my eye fills with tears. I wipe it roughly, impatient with my fluctuating feelings. Lying back against the pillows, I turn my head to gaze out at a clear blue sky.

❦

No one here has ever told me to look at myself. I have made my fast glances into the mirror, but nothing more. I can only take in so much at once. Today, after my shower, I stand naked in front of the mirror, leaning against the cold edge of the sink. For the first time, I allow my eye to focus on the emaciated apparition reflected back at me.

My hair is gone. It's been cropped right to the roots. My entire head is crisscrossed with suture lines. Tiny black suture-ends poke up here and there, between patches of dried blood. Every day the nurses work at the mess and try to clean it off, but my scalp is tender and I can't tolerate much. I'm amazed at how tough the old blood is. I can't see the back of my head, but I have been told the tissue there is dead. It still has floppy rubber drains protruding from it. Tomorrow they will remove the tissue. The fourth surgery since I've been here.

I lower my eye to my face. I remember seeing a large black

triangle in the middle of my forehead during one of my early side-long glances at the mirror. It was a piece of skin that was sewn back into place during the first operation and then died a few days later from a lack of blood supply. The doctors have removed it, pulling the skin together to close the gap. The mirror shows a suture line branching across my forehead. It is taut, causing me to frown. Tiny black stitches used to dot the angry red incision.

My right eye turns to the left, my bad eye. My left eyelids are gone. Skin from my inner arm and a muscle graft cover the damaged eyeball. A slit cut in the graft is the new opening, and only the tiniest little spot of eye is reflected there. I can't see out of my left eye at all. It's tight with scar tissue inside, and I can't move the graft. It just sits there for now, because the doctors aren't sure how it will heal. I protect the cornea with drops and ointment.

Poor eye. Under it, my face is sunken and flat. The left cheek-bone is missing, on the ground somewhere or inside the bear. They tell me they'll make a new cheekbone with a piece of rib one day.

My good eye has suture lines across the upper and lower lids, joining at and crossing my nose twice. Scar tissue pulls my eye sharply in, giving me an angry expression. Red ridges stretch from my ear to under my chin. Inside my mouth, rows of dissolvable sutures hold my lips on. My mouth is sore and can't seem to rid itself of the taste of blood. My lips don't move like they used to. My broken jaw is painful. Everything is swollen, and the areas that don't hurt are numb or tingly with unpleasant sensations of nerve regeneration. Hundreds of tiny stitches have patched together this puffed and funny-looking head.

My right eye takes this all in indignantly. I feel sick to my stomach. It hurts to look at myself, so why bother? How can anyone come into my room and tell me that I look good? It makes me furious.

What I see isn't even me.

❦

The trees outside my window are beginning to lose their leaves. I'm surprised. The last time I looked, they were brilliant with autumn colours. Today, the sky is grey and heavy. The trees careen in a strong wind. On the driveway in front of the hospital, people scurry from parking lot to entrance, their coats whipping around them.

I feel cheated. Sad. Cold world outside. Beige hospital world inside. What am I doing here?

My room is stuffy. The air vent hums in front of the window, fluttering the curtains. I have a fan, too. It blows the heat off my body. I always feel so hot.

I could leave. Go downstairs to the main entrance. Go sit on a park bench to cool off and watch wheelchair, visitor, handivan, ambulance, staff, in and out, door open and close, over and over.

Then I wouldn't have to look at the meal tray or lie in my yellow bed with its yellow sheets, yellow spread, yellow pillow with orange antiseptic spots on it from my new head dressing. Gauze-soaked medicine packing fills the raw hole where the back of my scalp used to be, wrapped all around with a gauze turban. I could put on some jeans, a heavy sweater, a windbreaker, and stand in the outside air. Pretend I was waiting for someone. Not be hurt or feel so weak. Not be this skinny person at the window, looking out.

Behind me, the door is open. I close my eye and focus on the sound. The addressograph machine at the desk is like a big stapler. Kechunk, kechunk. In the burn unit, someone yells. A cart rumbles along the hall. I hear the click, click, click of high heels walking by. The voices at the nurses' station rise and fall. Sometimes there's laughter. The nurses are a happy group; they bring warmth and brightness to my bland room.

The old lady down the hall starts to call for help. Again. I hate it. There have been weeks of it. Get rid of her; my head hurts. Poor old lady. Does anyone ever visit you? I wish I could go in and see you. The nurses are busy, and you demand a lot. It would make me feel good to help them, give you some company. But would you scream for help if someone looking like me walked in? You wouldn't know that I am a nurse dressed as a patient. What if you fought me, with my strange-looking head and face?

Trevor's blender starts up next door. He must be making

himself a snack to sip through a straw. Above the motor, I hear voices. Visitors. The blender is shut off.

Across the hall, they're running the tub. The big tub. I feel my stomach tighten. Who is the poor guy? His burns need debriding. They pull the dead skin off. When the water stops running, they will bring him in. He has a name; did something else before he came here to be a patient, before a few minutes of accident disfigured him. When I hear his stretcher coming, that's my cue to leave. I still have a moment.

The man is bathed several times a day. His pain comes into my room even through two closed doors. I can't stand to hear it. The first few times I felt sick. Not thinking of him: all I knew was that someone was yelling "No, No," and in my darkened world I was transported back to the hike out. The bear crashing through the bush to get to me, enormous paws thudding on the forest trail, hard animal eyes seeking me out.

The water shuts off. The stretcher clickety clicks by, into the tub room. Quickly, I'm away from the window and out of my room, heading for the solarium.

❦

We're escaping together, but Trevor won't say where we're going. He wants to get off the third floor so that we can be together without constant interruptions. He brought me a wheelchair and sat me in it, saying, "Don't ask. I want to show you something."

So here I am, being propelled along. My IV pole is between the footrests, and I balance it with one hand as the wheels roll over the floor tiles, then into the elevator. Trevor pushes. We wait in silence as the elevator descends. I sit with my head swaddled in gauze, my left eye buried under a thick white patch, hunched into my terrytowel housecoat, tissue in hand. Trevor takes me slowly down the ground-floor hallway, past the open doors of the staff cafeteria. Pastel- and white-uniformed staff dot the tables in clusters of three and four.

We're passing the personnel office and the job board. Slow and steady, Trevor pushes on.

"I feel as if it's been years since I sat in that cafeteria," I say. "I feel alien. Like I'm in another world entirely."

Silence.

"Do you know what I mean?"

"Yup." His voice is quiet.

We proceed without speaking to the wide side-by-side glass doors of a back entrance. Trevor parks the wheelchair facing west.

"See?" He is still speaking very quietly.

The clear evening light is on our faces. Past the radio-tower hill, the highway travels fifty miles to the mountains. Their snowy tops are distinct in the setting sun. Late autumn colours spread blanketlike before us.

"The mountains. So close." I turn my head to Trevor to smile my appreciation, but he has his back to me, pulling the glass doors wide open. A blast of cold air funnels through the doorway. I close my eye and breathe.

"Let's go outside for a minute." He's already behind me and pushing, pausing to steal my slipper to place between door and jamb. "It would be a long walk around, Trish," he says, momentarily playful.

I laugh up at him. The cold air creeps up my legs and into the arms of my housecoat. I shiver, wiping my right eye clear, and gaze at the panorama.

"I like it."

Trevor raises his fingers to hold his lips apart. "Look how clearly you can see Mount Lougheed. And it's had so much snow."

"Trevor? Are you sad tonight?"

He glances away, then back at me. "I'm just feeling quiet."

I nod, still shivering. "I'm tired. And cold."

"Let's go back, then." He turns the wheelchair quickly and pushes it through the doors, stopping to retrieve my slipper, then moving across bumpy tile. At the end of the long cafeteria hallway is a full-length mirror. A group of staff walks towards it, adjusting belts and slips and hair. They turn right towards the elevators, and Trevor and I are alone.

I see two patients reflected ahead of us, their width distorted at this distance, shapes growing larger as they approach the mirror. The woman in the wheelchair is slouched and bandaged. The man pushing her is tall and thin, with an uneven beard and a swollen face.

"Let's take stock, Trish."

Trevor stops the wheelchair abruptly in front of the mirror, then inches me forward until my slippered toes touch the glass. We scrutinize ourselves. Trevor puts his hand on my shoulder, and I reach one hand up to hold his fingers.

"What a wreck." It's my voice. I stare at a pale face patched with reddened scars. The body in the chair is bent. I pull myself up, then turn my face to the face above me in the mirror. Trevor is staring at his reflection.

Reaching up to hold his lips open, he is subdued. "We really took a beating." His words are slurred.

I look at myself again, then back at Trevor. He's gazing down at me in the mirror, his face serious. His eyes don't soften or laugh. They don't roam my face and enjoy it, not like they used to. We are strangers at this moment, and I feel the gulf between us. I don't want him looking at me that way. The expression in his good eye is dark; his face is crooked and scarred.

Trevor smiles a little smile. "We don't look so hot anymore, you know." This time his voice has an element of jest in it. He crosses his eyes, and we laugh.

Trevor pulls the chair away from the mirror, whirling it

around the corner to the elevators. Stabbing at the up button, he says, "I want to go ice climbing." I reach for his hand behind me, but he has moved away and stands facing a display case on the wall. He speaks again, his voice almost a whisper. "I've had enough of this place."

I feel the energy drain from me. It's replaced with desolation I can't push away. I don't know what to tell him. I don't know what to tell myself. I slump into the chair, anxious to get back to my room and my familiar yellow bed.

❧

It's been four weeks and I haven't seen the kids yet, my nephews and niece. Christopher is twelve, Graham eleven, Colleen ten. My oldest brother, Gordon, is their father. He comes to my room to tell me they are here. Do I want to go down to the lobby for a short visit? Yes. I'm so tired tonight, but I do want to see them. And I want them to see me, so that I can stop whatever is going on in their imaginations. I was mauled by a grizzly, and the whole side of my head could be missing, for all they know. People seem relieved when they actually see me, though I don't feel relieved when I see myself. I wish Trevor could come along with me, but he has gone over to the med school this evening. Too bad. The kids like him.

I link my arm with Gordon's. In the elevator, I sense stares directed at me. Beside my tall and solid brother, I am rail-thin and weak. My head feels big. Not as big as it did a few weeks ago, but still big and sore and not mine.

There they are, sitting in the main foyer. Christopher is expressionless and peering. Colleen looks uncomfortable. Graham launches himself from his chair and comes running over to us, dodging chairs and people. Dark blond hair, big smile, winter coat and boots.

"Patricia!" He slides abruptly to a halt on the polished floor in front of Gordon and me. His smile disappears. "Yuck! What happened to your *face!?*"

He begins an onslaught. "Why does your eye look like that? How come you have that bandage on your head? What happened to your forehead?"

"Hey, Graham. Just a minute. Let's go sit down." I point over towards the other two. I am cheerful. I like Graham's honesty. I would like to be as expressive and candid with myself. No pretending.

It's good to see these guys. Their shifting bodies perch on the edge of their chairs. Christopher, with dark eyes and hair, is growing up, getting taller and leaner all the time. He doesn't know whether to look at me or at his dad. He says hesitantly that he hopes I'll be feeling better soon. Colleen is silent, smiling shyly at me, her brown eyes uncertain, her leg-warmered legs wrapped tightly around the chair supports. I try to reassure them, launching into the explanations that Graham asked for: I look bad now, but I won't always look this way; I need another operation on my scalp, and that's why I'm wearing this wrap-around bandage; my eyes will look better after more surgery; I'm doing okay and am still the same Patricia inside. They listen carefully. We laugh at Graham's animated disgust as he hears that skin from my buttocks will be grafted to my scalp. "You'll have *bum* skin on your head?" he yelps.

Graham wants to know what they did with the bear. The kids like to camp and hike and spend time in the woods. I wonder what all this will do to that part of their lives.

Trevor has found us. He crosses the lobby floor with two of his classmates, all in their short white lab coats. The kids are hesitant, but he walks right in on our quiet little party and has big hellos and tickles for all three. Grabbing Graham, he turns him upside-down, daring him to try to get away. We laugh at my nephew's shrieks, and all around us people are glancing our way. We are a happy group. We are part of the world. I feel alive. Then, without any warning, the confusion and noise become too much for me. Trevor's friends want to talk, but I'm exhausted. I need to put my head down.

Usually, we end our visits with the kids with hugs and kisses, but will they want to this time? They give me stiff little hugs, looking over at their dad, and Colleen giggles. My face smiles while my head spins. I want my warm bed.

Trevor hugs each of the kids tightly, lifting them off the ground so that they cry out, laughing. With a last punch at Graham and a quick good-bye to his friends, he walks to the waiting elevator and me.

I watch him as he approaches. Trevor, my crooked man, with half a face that moves and half that remains impassive. His beard is growing back over his scars. His hair is growing back, too. His face is still swollen and puffed out on one side, and his jaw is wired shut. He looks funny, and I laugh at him. He wraps his arm around my waist and scowls down at me, pretending to be insulted.

"Who's laughing at who, numbskull wife?" He taps gently on the side of my head that has no sensation.

I'm so grateful to have that arm around my waist, that distorted face looking down at me, and Trevor behind it all, being Trevor again. I'm in hospital gown and housecoat. A patient. He's in jeans and a plaid shirt under his lab coat. A patient too, but an impatient one. He has an ear infection, but he's definitely healing. Although I'm also healing, I've got more surgery to go. I wish I was feeling as strong and as optimistic and as well as Trevor is now.

We stay close beside each other, holding hands all the way back to our rooms.

Today might be sunny, and that would be wonderful. These leaden skies are tiresome. Breakfast over, I sit in my orange upholstered chair and look out on the world. My hospital room is my private retreat. Visiting hours don't start till eleven, so this is my time alone. The nurse will be in soon to do my head dressing, but I have a few minutes to sit and think. I feel calm, at peace somehow. I'm thankful for that, though there's no way to predict how long the feeling will last.

Steve Herrero, an environmental biologist who studies grizzlies, came to see Trevor and me yesterday. Steve had been called in by Parks Canada to help investigate our attack. Yesterday was the first time Trevor and I had talked about it with anyone, including each other.

According to Steve, we'd walked into a loaded situation on our hike. A bighorn sheep with pneumonia had died seventy-five feet off the trail; the strong smell we noticed was no doubt the rotting carcass. The bear must have been feeding there when we came along the next day. Trevor and I weren't interested in that smelly thing, but bears will defend carcasses violently, and this one did. Perceiving us as a threat, she used her powerful jaws to break ours. That's how bears incapacitate their opponents.

Steve asked if we'd seen any ravens circling as we hiked. That would have been a clue to the presence of a dead animal. He asked about the wind, and I remembered that it had been blowing in my face. So the bear didn't get our scent, because we were downwind. Were we making any noise? Yes. We'd been talking and laughing, and Trevor was singing. She probably knew we were there long before we knew she was.

The bear would have taken my eye contact with her as a challenge, Steve said. Even so, she was unusually aggressive. Another bear in the same situation might have just bluff-charged to scare us away, and most grizzlies can't climb trees. But this one could, and she was enraged. She had two cubs, too, but we didn't see them. Steve told us they were nearly the size of their mother, almost three hundred pounds.

The grizzly charged the group of five men, including Steve, who went in to trap and move her out of the area. They killed her in self-defence. Otherwise, Trevor and I would have had company on this plastic surgery unit.

Trevor and I spoke quickly, filling in different parts of the story. I hadn't realized that he'd been attacked twice. At first, all he saw was a brown head flying at him through the bushes. He heard underbrush breaking, then barely had time to step back and half turn away before she was on him, all in seconds. He literally didn't know what had hit him. The two of us sat close as we talked with Steve. It was good to feel connected, and cathartic to share our experiences. But I was trembling the whole time.

A cart trundles past my room. "I'll be in in a few minutes, Patricia," the nurse calls through my partly closed door. No hurry. I hate these dressing changes of antiseptic-soaked packing in the missing scalp at the back of my head. I'm supposed to hop in the shower first, try to clean away some of the dried blood we are still fighting with. But I don't want to get up from my chair. I like sitting and mulling. The world outside my window is busy with traffic and people coming and going, but I'm safe and warm here in my cocoon.

When will it all seem real? Us, mauled by a grizzly. I'd thought about bears every time I went on a hike, but I never expected that I would actually be attacked. What are the chances? One in two million. I can't believe it. I don't *want* to believe it. Trevor says we got the best end of the deal. We lived, and the bear was shot. That doesn't really make me feel any better, my dear crooked man.

My calm is going to leave me unless I change my train of thought. I'll start to shake inside, then get irritable trying to control the anxiety. And I will end up crying. Again. I would like to stay in control today. I'd like to stay relaxed, and get that ever-ready picture of the bear flying at Trevor out of my head. Maybe I'll take a walk around the unit as a diversion.

The big wooden door to my room swings open easily, and the noises of the unit surround me. My legs are playing noodle. I hold on to the door frame for a minute, then head down the long hallway to the solarium, past the nurses' desk. Through open and half-open doors, I see feet under bed covers and patients washing up at sinks. The yellow-and-orange plaid curtains have been pulled open in each room to let the morning in. Dr. Lewis and the resident are doing rounds. Dianne is with them. I'll be back in my room before they get there. Their visit is the high spot of the day. I can ask questions, find out what will be next on my treatment agenda. Joke around some. The visit gives me something to go on, a connection with my future.

In the solarium, two old men are sitting and smoking. Awful smell, and the smoke burns my eyes. My pace quickens. I'm aware that I'm bent over like a sapling in the wind. Stand up straight. Don't be ashamed. Smile your funny face at people. Sometimes they smile back and stop staring. The burn patients get stared at, too. I'm walking past their area now, then back around to my room.

The dressing cart is parked at the foot of my bed. My sister Margaret, eight months pregnant and visiting from Edmonton, sits in my orange chair. I am happy to see her. Trevor has been visiting with her, perched on the edge of my messy morning bed, and he sends me his swollen half-grin. They will help me with my shower, and we will laugh about something, and the shower won't hurt so much. They will stay through the dressing and we will talk and it won't seem to take as long. Lisa comes in right behind me. She's my nurse today, short and dark and full of energy. She teases Trevor about the enormous breakfast he's consumed of pancakes, sausages, porridge and stewed prunes, all run through the blender and then sucked up through his straw.

Morning sunlight fills the room. Today won't be so bad. My supports are here. How could I ever feel alone?

☙

At home, Trevor and I would place a chair in the middle of the kitchen linoleum. He would sit, fidgety and talkative, while I moved slowly around him, combing and snipping. Cutting his hair was like trimming a curly brown hedge. But today, afraid that I might snip my IV tubing or his earlobe, he went to the barbershop. As he comes now to stand at the end of my bed, laughter and horror compete to surface within me.

"Trish, look!" His fingers hold his paralyzed lips open so he can speak. He cocks his head to one side, looking comically miserable. As he turns around in front of me, I laugh uncontrollably.

Above the level of his ears, his scalp shows white through brushcut bristles of hair. The hair on the top of his head is untouched; his long, unruly curls are pulled to the front and shaped into a curlicue. He had trimmed his beard before going, and the shortness of beard and hair on both sides of his head accentuate grotesquely the irregularities of his facial contours and expression.

"That was a butcher, not a barber. Poor you."

He leans towards the mirror to look at his reflection. He moans. "I went to that barber in the shopping centre," he says mournfully. "I planned to tell the guy just to take a little off all around. You know how it was long on top and uneven on the sides where they cut it to suture my scalp? But they were all staring at me like I was some kind of freak, with my puffed grapefruit cheek and Frankenstein suture lines. And before I could tell the guy what I wanted, he whipped the drape around me. With my hands pinned under there, I couldn't reach up to hold my lips open. So when he said, 'You want a trim?' all I could say was 'Hmifmmm.'"

He raises one eyebrow as he acts out the scene. I can't stop laughing, and I'm enjoying the deep release.

"So the barber picks up the electric razor and starts in on the back of my head. When he spun the chair around, I couldn't see the mirror anymore, so I just sat and listened to the ZZZZZttt. He must have thought I was a punk or something, Trish. He spun me back around at the end and asked, 'How's that?' I couldn't believe it. Then he took the bib off and said, 'That's eight dollars,' and I paid him and got out of there as fast as I could. I just need a safety pin for my ear now."

"Oh Trevor! You look terrible."

He moves to sit beside me on the bed. I look up at him with my good eye, leaning into his warmth.

"So next time you'll let your one-eyed wife do the job?"

His face twists into a smile, his good eye sparkly with humour. "We'll see."

Tomorrow I go back to the operating room again. Surgery number five. The nurse has told me they will take a muscle from my back, the latissimus dorsi, and graft it to the back of my head. They will need to transplant blood vessels with the muscle. Finely sliced sections of skin from my buttocks will cover the muscle graft. It's a tricky surgery, and I may be in the OR for as long as twenty hours.

Dread enfolds me. Another struggle to wake from the anaesthetic, more pain, more nausea. I want to get strong now. I am so tired of fighting. I don't want to be a patient anymore.

The back of my head is bone now; only bone. During my showers this past week, my hand sometimes slipped into what felt like an awesome cavity. The thought, the memory torments me. I hadn't realized the scalp is so thick. My skull. I touched it. I could take care of the same injury on someone else, but somehow, because this is my head, I can't handle it. I want the nurse to tell me that I will be up and around and feeling just fine in a couple of days. But she doesn't. Each plastic surgery is so different. She can't reassure me.

Late that evening, I lie in bed wrapped up in doubt and worry. I'm coiled. Tight. When a crepe-soled nurse comes in with pills on a little tray, I take them eagerly. I sleep, but wake again in the middle of the night.

Nightmares. Can't close my eye because of nightmares. The bear bites down on my face, leaving a bloody hole. I'm crying, frightened. The night is dark behind my curtains. I want so much to be in control, but I am losing it.

The nurses debate out at the station. I worry that they are tired of me. A nurse with a pretty face and soft brown hair brings a little paper cup with a pill in it. It's something else this time. She comes to the edge of my bed, offering me her hand. Sits with me and talks for a minute. I want to bury my head in her lap and weep, but she is impatient. The pill takes over.

When I wake again, it is early. Weak light filters into the room. I go to the operating room at eight. What time is it now? I hear talk at the desk: shift change. Low voices, low laughter. I lie under thin sheets awaiting my premedication.

There's a knock at the door, then a head looks around the corner. It's Dr. Lewis. He sits beside me on the bed, his hands deep in lab-coat pockets.

"I heard you had a bad night?" His eyes rest calmly on my face. He is solid, real, dependable. An ally. But fear sits heavily in me. Even with him there, the morning is cold and unfriendly. Sitting up, I reach over awkwardly and hold on to him. Bury my sobbing in his shoulder. I have surprised him, but his arms come around my back, and one hand pats it awkwardly. I feel foolish. Yet I cling, hearing my voice saying over and over, "I'm so scared." It is a relief to say it, to have him know.

When I feel calmer, I pull my knees up and hold on to them

with long thin arms. I ask Dr. Lewis to clarify what the nurses have told me. How will I feel afterward? How long will the surgery take? I shiver as my words fly. He listens without interrupting, but I can tell from his expression that he has gone over all this with me before. It didn't register then. Somehow I am able to absorb it now. He's the one who should be nervous, he finishes; he's got a big job ahead of him. I want to laugh. My mouth won't even smile, but I feel better. With a brief touch of my hand, he is gone.

The noises from the hall increase, and the nurse is here. She has a needle on a small green plastic tray. I'm surprised at the amount of morphine the anaesthetist has ordered, yet I crave its effect. I have washed and put on a clean blue gown, and I shift onto my side for the injection.

Within moments, a thin veil is pulled over my mind. It's difficult to keep my eye open, and my mouth is dry and tacky. It's impossible to feel afraid. Carefree, I drift.

I'm outside the operating room. How did I get here? I vaguely remember wiggling onto a stretcher. I feel fear hiding behind the drug, trying to get at me. My IV drips beside my left arm.

I stare at the square of fluorescent lighting above me. This is the floor I used to work on. How many times have I dropped patients off here and told them "I'll see you later"? I always thought they would like to hear that. Sometimes, I would touch a hand or shoulder or foot before leaving.

A pink OR uniform stands by my right arm. With a great

effort, I turn my head and focus on a friendly face above me. A warm female hand takes mine.

"It won't be long," she tells me.

I try to talk, but my mouth is too dry and cakey. I relax, close my eye. There is bustle in the background, machinery hum and hiss.

Then my stretcher moves. Down a hall. Into the OR. I've seen this movie before.

The narrow table is hard and cold. The room is shiny beige tile. Hoses and dials and lights surround me. Capped, masked people move in and out, sky blue and drab hospital green. A male voice behind a mask tells me they'll need to start another, larger IV. He avoids eye contact, says they will give me a local anaesthetic first.

Oh no. To my drugged eye, the IV catheter looks like someone's garden hose. My body tightens. Don't hurt me.

But they do. They miss the vein.

There is a hand to squeeze on my left side. I use it. I lie naked under a thin sheet and gown, with a confusion of bodies around me. The room is cold. Then the IV is in. Why does it still hurt?

A voice comes from behind my head. "We're going to put you to sleep now."

Panic. No! I try to see the voice. Faces float above me. Silently, Dr. Lewis appears, standing shorter than the other bundled bodies waiting around the table. All I can see are his eyes between blue mask and cap.

"I'm scared." I peer up through a fog, tilting my head to focus on him.

"I know." An instant's warm hand pressure.

That's it. My muscles release. You can put me to sleep now. He knows. And cares. I'm ready. I'm gone.

I'm almost awake. My tongue and the inside of my mouth are made of tissue paper. My lips are swollen and parched. I can't lick them. The recovery room is bright through my closed eyelid. I can't open my good eye. Why?

Someone moans. And moans again. It's me.

A drink. I try to say it. The sound is incomprehensible. I drift off. Wake again. I've got to get off my right side. That arm hurts.

"Waaer." A hand presses firmly on my shoulder and tells me not to move. The voice is impatient. Sharp. I call out that I want a drink. No answer. I hear footsteps and voices all around me. There's something wrong with my arm, they say. Someone tells someone else to call the doctor.

My mouth is going to fall off and blow away if I don't get a drink. I want to move. I feel so heavy. I try yelling.

"Relax, dear." Squeaky nurse shoes come close, then walk away.

I'm angry. Why won't anyone listen to me? I struggle to sit up. Have just barely moved when along comes the firm hand again.

"Don't you move. We're trying to get hold of the doctor for you. Lie down and stay there."

I garble.

"What do you want?"

I tell her slowly and carefully. I can't see her, but I know she's in front of me.

"No! You're not allowed to drink anything." She sounds exasperated.

I'm mad. Groggy mad. I try to sit up again. That will get me some attention. Instantly, another voice. Quiet and calm. A gentle pressure on my shoulder.

I bellow. "Water!" It is a croak, but more like the word than any try so far.

She's gone, then back. Something wet comes into contact with my lips. "I can't give you a drink. Can you suck on this?" A cold, wet washcloth. Delicious. Heaven. My mouth is almost a mouth again.

Another voice tells me apologetically that the doctor says I have to stay in this position in spite of the pressure on my arm. My arm? Who cares about my arm? I've got my mouth back. I float off, leaving the bright lights and busy noises behind.

I'm back in my room, from the sound of things. In my bed. I ache. There are people in my room, fussing about. I feel awful. I can't see. My eye is swollen shut again. Good. I'm glad. I don't want to wake up. I don't want to tell anyone how I'm feeling. I can shut the world out. Stay alone in my misery.

But someone wants my attention, is calling me softly from far away. My name. Patricia. It's Dr. Lewis, I think. Telling me something.

I concentrate hard. My mind fuzzes over, clears, then fuzzes again.

". . . the lump on the side of your head will go away. It will take a few months, but the swelling will go down." His voice carries on, but I can't stay here. Can't catch the rest. I'm drifting.

Lump on my head.

When I wake again, it's dark. I struggle to move. Oh God. I hurt. Hurt. Hurt. I whimper.

My mother's voice comes from behind me. "I'm here, Patricia."

Mom! I hate this. Get me out. Help me. It's so dark again.

"What time is it?" Dry-mouth words.

"Eleven o'clock, dear." Softly.

"How many days since my surgery?"

There's a moment's hesitation. "You had your surgery yesterday. It took twelve hours."

Her voice is so gentle. My mind tries to work. Yesterday? Impossible! It's been weeks. I'm sure of it. At least a few days. Only yesterday? Just the beginning? I can't do it. Can't take it anymore. Lead-weight misery.

"Mom. What am I going to do?"

Dr. Lewis's words come back to me. Lump on the side of my head.

I raise my arm. Ouch. Spasms. Horrible spasms. How much muscle did they take? Slowly, inch by inch, I move my hand up to my head, gritting my teeth against the pain. The side of my head. Breathe deeply. Touch.

What the hell is it?

A lump? That's not a lump! It's a mountain. Attached to my head, warm and throbbing. What did they do to me?

I sink and sink and sink. My mind shuts off. Don't think. He said it will go away. Think about it later. Not now. Crying inside. Never mind. Go to sleep. In sleep there is escape.

❦

A nurse speaks in my dim morning room. I've got to go up to the ninth floor for something to do with my left eye, she tells me. It's not seven o'clock yet. It's still dark out. Leave me alone.

The doctor is waiting, she says, and they want me right now. A new eye doctor, a corneal expert. She pauses expectantly.

I don't want to see another eye doctor. I like the one I've got.

Can I walk to my appointment? the nurse wants to know. No. Not this morning. She fetches a wheelchair.

"Get up, now."

I haul my baggy blue-gowned self out of bed. Drag myself into the chair. I can't keep my eye open, and it still hurts so much to move, even though it's almost a week since my surgery. I want something to put on the back of my head. Don't want the world staring at my puffy new scalp and the swollen purple lump of tissue above my left ear. My punk doorknob, I call it. I hate its weirdness.

We place a sterile white towel over my head like a kerchief. Disguised, I slouch in the chair, head down, eye shut, letting the trip happen to me.

Nurses coming to work are talking at the passenger elevators. We take the service ones. Good. I don't want to see anyone I know this morning. I applied for a transfer to the ninth floor just before our accident. The head nurse there knows me, and she might be around. I hope not. Let's just get this over with so I can go back to bed.

The nurse parks me at the desk on the ninth floor. I've parked patients like this myself, many times. As I wait for someone to come and get me, I sit with my head down. Silently, my wheelchair is turned, and I'm taken to a little windowless room at the end of the hall. I'm placed in a chair in front of a machine that I don't like the looks of. Don't come near my sore eyes with that.

The doctor has glasses and he's smiling, but he doesn't really look at me. He's certainly awake. *Too* awake. His voice is bright. He wants me to put my chin here and make my eye look through there. A light flashes. Ouch! I want to cry. I fight to hold still as I am supposed to. I'm tired of crying. I won't. The doctor is talking, humming to himself.

He's done. I can go. But wait, he's still talking. I don't want to listen. What's he saying? My left eye will never see again, will never move again, never have a functioning eyelid again. And more. My mind shuts him out. I'm wrapped in despair. And so tired.

He takes me back to my wheelchair, and then I don't hear him anymore. I'm wheeled to the desk, where I sit and wait, shivering. Someone from the third floor will come and get me.

The hospital is waking up. A misty cold light comes through the windows. Dully, I sit counting my IV bruises and examining the bear scars on my right hand. I am surprised at how fast they are healing. Footsteps behind me, and my wheelchair moves. There's no attempt at conversation. Either my mood shows, or someone else is in a bad mood this morning too. Fine with me.

I am parked silently at my room door, then I walk, feeling shaky, to my bedside table. I look for my custom felt-penned "Do Not Disturb" sign. I don't want visitors this morning. I don't want people popping in to say hi and telling me how wonderful I look and how it could have been worse and how well I'm doing. Not today. I don't feel like being nice today. I tape the sign to the outside of my door and retreat.

My room is hot and welcoming. The drapes are drawn and

the room is almost dark. My bed is askew, just as I left it. I crawl in. Pull the covers up tight. Something inside of me curls up, and I am cut off from the hospital world out there. Alone with my thoughts. I'm too exhausted to keep them away.

Mauled by a grizzly. I let my mind taste the words. It's not supposed to happen. Trevor and I did things right.

I want to sleep, but in the morning dim, sleep is far from me.

Wilcox Pass. It was one of the summers when Trevor and I worked in a campground at the north end of Banff Park. One gorgeous sunny day we went for a hike, rambling through flowering alpine meadows. At a wide copse of wind-twisted subalpine firs, the trail split. Trevor wanted to explore, suggesting that I take one fork and he the other. We could keep in touch with each other by yodelling, he said, and we could see if the trails joined up again. I wasn't convinced it was a good idea, but I shelved my hesitancy and agreed.

Trevor's trail went uphill to the left. Mine continued straight ahead. He yodelled. I yelled back and kept walking. The bush was thick and silent except for the sound of my boots along the trail. Another yodel. I yelled back, hoping our paths would soon join up.

I started as a bird fluttered out of the bush beside me. I was relieved to see a meadow ahead. With Trevor yodelling from somewhere above me in the thick trees, I stood at the edge of the meadow, yelling back. Bees and bugs droned around me. Trevor's yodels echoed through and through the peaks surrounding us, with silence in between. I began to get impatient. He should have reached the meadow by now. His voice always seemed to be coming from the same spot. What could he be doing? Listening to the echoes? Playing? I paced on my spot, yelling back, angry now.

"Trevor! Come down! Let's go!"

The day was hot. Huge bothersome horseflies swirled around. I swatted at them, furious, and glared up at the trees. Finally I stomped off across the meadow, following the trail but staying in the open. From behind me another yodel and its rallying echo sounded. My voice was hoarse as I stood and screamed Trevor's name up at the trees.

"Trevor! Answer me! Come down now!" As loud as I could, spacing the words for emphasis. No response.

I continued with firm steps to the other end of the meadow, muttering under my breath. Another damned yodel cut the quiet. The trail disappeared into trees again here, heading downhill and back out to the highway. I waited, fuming, with arms crossed. It had been at least an hour since we'd split up, and no more than a ten-minute walk through the copse where I was. My eyes searched the heavy forest.

Suddenly — what's that?

My eyes were drawn sideways to a spot along the edge of the trees, halfway between Trevor's trail and mine. A figure shoved out of the bushes with long strides, arms pumping, moving fast. Trevor's face as he neared me was full of fury. His feet hit hard on the soft turf, and his head was thrust stiffly forward, jarring with each step. I drew back in amazement.

"Why didn't you answer me? What were you doing up there?" My voice cracked as I yelled. How dare he be mad?

"Why the hell didn't you answer *me?* Where have *you* been?"

His face glared hotly inches from mine, and I felt a surge of indignation. "I've been yelling till I almost lost my voice!"

All of a sudden, I realized we were fighting. We'd never raised our voices at each other before. Never been so angry. It surged within me.

"I don't like being left alone with the horseflies while you play around with your stupid yodels!" At a loss for words, I sputtered into quiet.

Trevor's arms moved as if to grab me, and he leaned closer, his eyes spitting fire.

"I didn't hear you! I didn't hear you yelling! Yells don't carry through the trees. You have to yodel. I've told you that before. I didn't hear you, you idiot, and I've spent the last hour combing the bush. I thought a bear got you!"

I watched his face in amazement. There were little twigs in his hair. His voice quieted abruptly, and he moved his face a few inches back, still fixing me with an intent glare.

"I was worried about you, Trish. I was looking for your body. Why didn't you answer me?"

Not finished with my own anger, I yelled back. "I *did!* Over and over."

With a look of total disgust, he stomped away down the trail, my voice pursuing him.

"Trevor! I didn't know you couldn't hear me!"

I listened to my own fast breathing, shaking my head. Looking for my body. He thought a bear had attacked me.

A bear? Me? Ha!

The memory of that hike is still so vivid. The anger. Trevor's frantic concern. I was fearful then of the strength of our emotion. But I couldn't conceive of being attacked.

Someone is at my door with a breakfast tray. I'm yanked back to the hospital world as the smell of egg rises in front of me. I don't want to eat. But I will. I will get better, and I will go home. I will see out of this eye again. I will have eyelids and my eye will move and it will be a pretty blue. I will look just like I used to.

❧

Trevor and I have permission to go out on a pass. It's over a month since our accident. It feels as if we've been in here much, much longer, and I am terrified to go back out into the world.

My parents arrive to pick us up. We'll go to their place for a short visit. Dad waits out front with the station wagon while my mother stands quietly in the doorway to my room, waiting for me to put on my shoes. This has been such an ordeal for her. She's waited patiently through my surgeries, always beside my bed in case I should wake or ask for something or need to talk. She's brought special soups and milkshakes and puddings to tempt my appetite. I look at her as I stand to put on the warm winter coat she has brought for me. She has big hazel eyes and a gracious, kind face. Tonight she appears relaxed and happy as she looks back at me. Her wavy black hair has more grey in it than I remember. I bend to give her a hug at the door. Arms linked, we go to collect Trevor.

He's in his room, lying on the bed in a sweatsuit, wearing a big lopsided grin. Taking my other arm as we start down the long tiled hall, Trevor sings through his wired jaw, his hand held to his lips to hold them apart.

"We're off to see the Wizard, the wonderful Wizard of Oz." He's in high spirits tonight. I like to see him happy. He has his down times and an occasional good cry, but he says he feels lucky and glad to be alive in spite of everything. He tries a hop with his song, sending me jolting into Mom. Ouch. Lucky! That word has no place in my vocabulary just now. But though I can't match Trevor's enthusiasm and energy, I revel in a quiet excitement about my own progress.

In the elevator, people examine us closely. It's the same old story. I feel them looking so I turn to look back, to smile and show them that I am human; they turn away quickly to pretend they weren't looking. I feel like wearing a sign saying "A bear did it." A man in the lobby stares openly. I smile into his goggle eyes. But his expression remains unchanged, and he swivels his head to follow us out the front door. Thanks, mister. Everyone tells me how good I look. Liars. I keep my face to the ground as we leave the hospital.

Dad hurries around to the back passenger door when he sees us. I bend cautiously and fold myself in, careful of my sore new scalp and back incision. It's difficult getting comfortable with the still-raw skin-donor sites on my rear end, but with some shifting I'm settled.

Trevor bounces in beside me, grabs my hand and holds it firmly. The expressive side of his mouth smiles at me, but his eye communicates sadness. Why is he looking at me like that?

"Are you happy, love?" His voice is hopeful. I nod, wanting to reassure him. He grips my hand more tightly. "I don't like people staring at you."

I would like to cuddle my head into his shoulder like I used to, but my broken facial bones won't let me. Instead, I take his hand in both of mine and we move closer together, shoulder to shoulder, thigh to thigh. There's a whole evening ahead of us, out and away.

Dad drives slowly, taking the corners with caution. I'm glad, because the bumps and turns hurt. What a wreck I am. I don't like feeling so weak, nor as vulnerable in the car as I do. I'm sure we're going to have an accident on the way to my parents' house. The world is big and full of disasters just waiting to get at us. The purpose of living seems only to stay alive.

It's crisp and cool, more than halfway through October. How incredible. The trees are leafless, but as we cross the Bow River, I see remnants of a beautiful autumn in the bushes all along the riverbanks. The freeway is busy with traffic, and things seem hectic and fast, but our street when we arrive is serene and quiet and safe. Tall cottonwoods line the road. As I get out of the car, the air nips cold on my face. It's as though I've been away for years, and I need to just stand and look for a moment. This is the house I grew up in. Its steep-pitched, red-shingled roof, white stucco walls and black-trimmed windows are familiar, comforting. The yard is clean, manicured for winter by Dad. A fat black squirrel jumps from a tree onto the garage roof and disappears into neighbouring bushes. I breathe deeply, then walk slowly up the brick and cement stairs. My Auntie Gerry, here for the evening, stands at the open front door, welcoming us in.

I curl up at one end of the comfortable old yellow-flowered chesterfield. I am chilled. Mom brings a bulky comforter and tucks it all around me, bending to kiss the top of my head before turning away. I'm overwhelmed. Everything is the same, but I am a stranger in some way. Take it slow, says the voice in my head.

Trevor is close beside me on the couch. Mom and Dad and Auntie Gerry sit in soft upholstered chairs, talking quietly and drinking tea. The yellow light from a corner lamp is mellow and friendly. The house is calm around us. I'm glad we came. I feel loved. I feel grateful to be alive and appreciative of my caring family. I feel thankful for a live, smiling, talking, singing husband. I am happy to sit and watch and feel. The world shrinks to a size I can handle in my parents' living room.

❧

There are several new admissions today. File folder charts lie across the nurses' station desk, waiting to be processed by the unit clerk. I am leaning against the counter, waiting for a nurse's attention. The top chart is for a Mr. Karl. I remember caring for a patient with that name last year, and I wonder if this is the same man. He was dying of stomach cancer, and he spent months on the surgery floor where I used to work. On Christmas Day, his hospital room was full of family and church friends singing soft hymns, with candles lit all around. Mr. Karl was a placid man with a strong German accent, a good sense of humour and a friendly face. He spoke of dying quite openly, more comfortable with his diagnosis than I was. I developed a deep respect for him.

"Do you need something, Trish?"

I look up. I recognize Leona in the blue of the unit clerk's uniform. Yes, she tells me, this could be the man I took care of. He's in Room 330. Why don't I go in and say hello?

Down the familiar beige hall I walk. Trevor and I have been here six weeks now, and I am much stronger. I wear the standard blue patient's gown and a flowered kerchief to hide my cropped hair and new scalp graft, but my eye is unpatched. I wonder how acceptable I look.

Outside the partially closed door to Mr. Karl's room, I am suddenly uncertain. He may not remember me. He may not recognize me. And if he is much sicker by now, maybe I shouldn't be bothering him by dropping in. I hesitate.

Through the open door I can see yellow bedclothes with two feet poking up under them. I stand in the entrance. There is a woman on the other side of the room.

"Is it all right if I come in?" The expression on her face tells me it isn't. The evening sky is framed in the window behind her.

"Come on in," says a hoarse voice.

A skinny, hollow-faced man smiles at me as I step inside. The bedclothes lie neatly over his small frame. The head of the bed is cranked up, and pillows prop up his body. It is the same Mr. Karl.

"I don't know if you will remember me. I'm Patricia. I took care of you last year . . . upstairs. I was a nurse there."

He nods. "I remember you. How are you and your husband?"

I'm surprised. He not only remembers me, he knows about our accident. He motions me to come closer.

"We're doing well. Much better. We'll be going home soon." Oh-oh. Was that the wrong thing to say to someone who will never be going home again? But no, I think. He will be happy to hear our good news.

"How are you doing?" My turn to ask him. The woman on the other side of the bed smiles nervously, reaching over to straighten the covers.

"I'm here to die this time." His tone is quiet and even, and his eyes don't leave my face. I don't know what to say. I nod.

"I'm ready." He moves slightly in the bed, grimacing. Dark urine drains into the catheter bag hanging from the bed. His IV drips steadily, joined by plastic tubing to a slender arm. His face is jaundiced. With a start, I realize how much he has deteriorated since the last time I saw him.

His eyes spark. "Did they ever get that bear? They should shoot all those bears. Something like this should never happen! They're crazy if they don't destroy them all."

"They did shoot the bear. The next day. She died. But we survived." I pause a moment. His eyes still show anger. "We just ran into bad luck. But we've had great care here and exceptional plastic surgery. We'll get better."

He's scowling, shaking his head. This is awkward. Maybe it was a mistake to come in. I don't want to talk about our attack.

It seems pointless to ask more about him, though. So what do we talk about?

"You know, I think I hate cancer almost as much as you hate bears."

He laughs, his face crinkling all over. "I am ready, though. I've accepted it. I have my family and my church. They are wonderful. I'm at peace."

Shifting again in bed, Mr. Karl tells me that his stomach feels uncomfortable. Glancing down at his catheter bag, I can see that the upper chamber is full to overflowing. The backup would be causing pressure on his bladder. Just as I move to open the valve that will allow urine to drain into the lower collecting chamber, a student nurse enters the room. She is blonde and pretty enough to be a nurse in a soap opera. She squats at the bedside, but the upper chamber won't drain, and urine leaks out onto the floor. A puddle forms at her feet. I know what the problem is. I stepped out of the way when she first entered, but I squat beside her now.

"It's formed an air lock. Do you want me to show you how to get rid of it?"

Mr. Karl is smiling, leaning to watch. His visitor has come around the bed, and with our four heads huddled over the bag, I explain the trick of releasing the air lock. The student nurse stands, wiping her hands lightly on her uniform, then turns to the sink to wash them. She goes off to get a mop.

As I stand at the sink to wash my own hands, I laugh at the

me I see in the mirror. Me, a patient. It is still so strange. It seems years since I wore a nurse's uniform and emptied a catheter bag. I want to get home and be a normal person again.

Mr. Karl has settled back on his bed. "That feels better. Thanks."

"I'm glad. I'll go now. I just want to wish you all the best."

"Thank you for coming in to see me."

We smile faint smiles. I wonder how calm he really is. It's so easy to feel depressed in here, and he won't be getting better. Impulsively, I offer my arms for a hug. His face is impassive, but his body responds. It feels frail and warm.

Mr. Karl's eyes close. In repose, all the lines of his face turn downward. His visitor stands with her back to us, looking out the window. Outside, the evening sky has turned dark.

My slippered feet are silent as I leave, pulling the door closed behind me.

❧

I lie curled on my right side, wide awake. Two A.M. The hospital is quiet. It's early November, seven weeks into our stay, and Trevor and I share a double room. We are far enough down the hall to be isolated from the noise of the nursing station. But my mind won't let me rest. Thoughts carry me in dizzy circles.

We found out today that we will be leaving the hospital sometime this week, and the prospect fills me with uncertainty. Does that mean we're better? I guess not. We're more capable, well enough to be sent home for now. We will both be back for more surgeries later.

I have permission to lie on the back of my head now, or on the left side where my head graft curves around and over my ear, but I can't. Those areas are still too tender. The raw squares on my arm and buttock are healing. I will do those donor-site dressings myself at home. My left eye needs to be taken care of until the next surgeries, and I'll be doing my own ointment and eye patches after discharge. They want me to start practising here, but I am resistant. It means looking at myself, at my eye, in a mirror. I have a feeling, somewhere in the pit of my stomach, that this will be even more difficult in my own bathroom mirror. Looking disfigured is acceptable in a hospital. I don't want to go home and face myself looking this way.

My hair is coming back, though not fast enough for me. I don't look shaved anymore, and the blood is all washed out, but scars crisscross the islands of my hair, and the bumps on my scalp disturb me. My right eye is not as angry-looking as it was, because the scars have softened a bit. I'm glad. I couldn't stand to see it so pulled and frownlike.

Trevor sleeps, breathing noisily across from me. I would like to relax like that. My head aches. From thinking? I am restless, tired of lying here. I wish I could sleep, but as soon as I start to drift off, my mind fills with pictures I don't want to remember, of the bear hurling herself at Trevor and up the tree to get at me. Then I jerk awake, heart pounding. When will the pictures stop? When will life just go on?

I decide to get up again. The floor is cold, and I grope with bare feet under the bed for my slippers.

The big wooden door squeaks as I pull it open. Light from the hall spills into the room. I turn to look at Trevor, almost hopeful that he will wake up. But his breathing doesn't change. Before he went to bed he played his guitar for me, and self-consciously, with mumbling lips, sang quiet songs. It wouldn't be fair to wake him now.

Slowly, with my housecoat pulled tightly around me, I walk to the desk. The nurses look up from their bright night island. Their faces are cheery. They all have suggestions. Would I like to sit with them for a while? Why don't I have a warm cup of something? Is there something I could read to relax? Nothing clicks. I walk on.

Misery has become my companion once again. What I'd really like is someone to talk to about my feelings. Someone I don't have to worry about hurting or burdening with my confusions and pains. I hate the grotesque way I look. It could be worse, I know. It could be better, too. I continue down the dim night hall. I'm so sick of these emotions. So sick of feeling exhausted.

There is a little bench at the telephones way down by the

elevators. I sit there and cry. The lights are bright around me. Maybe I could call my friend Laura in Ontario, but I don't know what time it is there, and I don't know if anyone has told her about our accident. I cry only from my right eye. There are no tears from the strangeness that is my left one. That makes me cry harder. I'm fed up with the crying, too, but I let myself sob. Finally, my tears slow down.

I head towards our room. On my way past the nurses' desk, I ask for more pills. No problem. Someone will bring them right in. Back in my warm bed, I pull my covers tight and wait. I'd like to talk for a moment with my nurse, but she doesn't seem to understand my need, and I'm too tired to explain it. Besides, if I poured out my feelings, I'd scare her away. I've tried before. Most of them reassure without listening.

When she's gone, I'm alone with Trevor's breathing once again. The dark is deep. The night is quiet. I sleep.

☙

Trevor and I are going home. We'll stay with my parents for the first few weeks, to ease the transition. The double room they gave us is beginning to look like any other hospital room. Our favourite messages have been taken down off the wall, packed into a box with the wonderful two-foot-high cards my nephews and niece made for us of a big, smiling, yellow sun and little brown deer in a forest. Many of the cards we got are from people we've never met.

The photos stuck up above our beds are also peeled carefully from the paint. The picture of me standing next to our friend Brent on the West Coast Trail last summer, my hair bleached blonde by the sun, both my eyes smiling and happy. A bigger picture of Trevor and Brent and me standing at the tailgate of Brent's old truck at the trailhead of Dolomite Pass in Banff National Park, my favourite hike. My face is angular and full of summer sunshine, my legs long and lean from cycling mountain roads to work. Trevor is between Brent and me, his eyes merry, his dark curls needing a trim. He's wearing the yellow- and green-striped rugby shirt that his family beg me to hide from him; its cuffs and collar are frayed and tattered. His arm is around my waist. There's another photo that Tim, a med-school friend, took of Trevor on Professor Falls, their last ice climb. Trevor's coming over the top edge, pick planted in the frozen waterfall, face wreathed in smiles. This is Trevor in his element. His icy beard and brows and hair are squished down under a warm winter tuque and a climbing helmet.

We have so many plants to take home with us, too. We load them with everything else onto a little hospital cart to take downstairs. It's like moving house; we've accumulated so much. I have to pack slowly or my heart gallops away on me and I'm out of breath in a flash. The sick-person role still catches me by surprise. I stop to look over at Trevor, who sits on his bed humming and sorting through an accumulation of papers. He glances up, surveying our emptying blue room.

"It's strange leaving, isn't it?" he asks me. His voice is quiet, his swollen face solemn. I nod and sit heavily on my bed.

"Lie down and take it easy, Trish. I can finish the rest."

I swing my legs up and put my head down on the yellow pillow.

"It will be good to get home, love," Trevor says. I nod, closing my eye to relax and listen to the hospital noises for our last few moments here. Trevor moves around me, checking in drawers and lockers. I do want to go home. I want to be with Trevor again in our little place. But I'm so scared of everything these days.

We wait for lunch before leaving. Trevor steals half my portion of lasagna, and it disappears into his blender with some hot water, to be made into mush he can drink with a straw. He's so determined to gain weight back that he inhales it, then goes to the kitchen to see what else there is. He comes back with a cellophane-wrapped piece of apple something and a Dixie cup of ice cream. Making smacking noises with his mouth, he heads for the blender. I have to laugh. I feel a sudden rush of gladness.

The room is stripped bare. It's just an empty hospital room now. Maybe it will be good to be at home again. Maybe.

Dianne's at the door. "I hear you've been looking for me." She's smiling. "You two are on your way?"

She feels small when I stand to hug her and give her the big thank-you's I feel. Tears from my right eye slide down my cheek to the corner of my mouth, and Dianne cries too, wiping roughly at her cheeks. With blurry smiles, we say good-bye.

The nurses at the desk are full of good wishes. More hugs. Trevor and I will be back for more surgery, but never like this. We're on our own again. We turn and walk down the hall, skinny and scared.

III

Home

❦

The pink-walled bedroom I had as a child is due for painting again. Trevor perches on the edge of the double bed, pulling his socks off. My parents' house is old, filled with dark wood trim. The floors squeak when you walk on them. I sit next to Trevor, feeling heavy and slow.

"It was weird to visit our own place today, wasn't it?"

He nods, not speaking.

"It feels like we've been away for years, not two and a half months. It's hard to believe it will be December soon." I pause, waiting to see if he'll comment, but he hasn't had much to say to me for the past couple of days. We argued yesterday; he told me that I'm dwelling too much on the accident, being too negative. I miss him. I miss us. I try again.

"Didn't you think our place felt empty and strange? I'm scared to go back there. I don't know what it will be like for us without the distraction of other people and things going on all the time. Two weeks here, at Mom and Dad's, has been so comforting."

He stands to take off the rest of his clothes, his thin, long body moving smoothly. That green-and-yellow rugby shirt. I don't really like it, but he's enamoured of it, impatient when it's in the wash. He climbs beneath the covers, still silent. I'm annoyed with him. I want to talk.

"Trevor, I can't go skiing with you tomorrow. I'm too tired. My muscles are gone. I need to do things slowly. I know you want to get right back at it and ski and ice climb and skate and hike. I feel like you're angry with me."

"I'm not angry," he responds sulkily.

"I just feel so terrified all the time, so vulnerable. I'm sorry, but I do. I don't want to be this way. I hate it. And I hate disappointing you."

I feel tears coming and I fight to hide them. Trevor's hungry for life and adventure again. It's like he needs to pretend what we've been through is no big deal. But even seeing snow-covered evergreens nauseates me. I want him to care about my fears. I want us to feel close.

"While we were outside today, I kept looking for the airplane that was going to crash on our heads. I worry all the time that something else is going to happen." I'm crying in earnest now as

I crawl into the old double bed. Trevor is curled tightly away from me. I place a hand on his shoulder, willing him to turn. He's motionless. I hear the low sound of my parents' voices in the hall. I could go out to my mother, but I don't want to upset her. It's obvious that Trevor and I are having trouble these days, and she's tied in knots about it.

Trevor's breathing is thick and difficult beside me. I cry harder, thinking of our faces. I hate his twisted, thickened nose, his contorted masklike look. He must hate it too. Why won't he admit that it bothers him? Is he denying it, or is he just that much stronger than I am?

❧

Dr. Lewis nods good-bye as we leave his office. It's our first visit to him as outpatients. "See you in two weeks," he says. He has a solid, composed presence, but my mind is turbulent with all the information he has given us.

It's six-thirty, and outside the hospital windows the sky is darkening quickly. It's time for us to go home to our suppers. It still seems strange not to have the reassurance of daily rounds. Trevor's jaw will be unwired next week in preparation for a December surgery to repair it. After that he will be able to talk without holding his lips apart. I would like to get another surgery out of the way too, and gain a sense of progress, but my injuries are different. I will have to wait until spring sometime, when my scars will have matured sufficiently. Dr. Lewis was pleased with the success of the graft on the back of my head, though. And he was encouraging about my damaged left eye, mentioning vague plans for the reconstruction of eyelids.

As Trevor and I walk along the hallway, two figures approach us. Our mirror reflections. We stop for a minute to look. The person I used to see in this mirror was a tall nurse in white uniform with a full head of thick, dark-blonde hair, her corduroy knitting bag over one shoulder. She would be returning to her surgical floor after a break, laughing with other nurses but thinking ahead to the rest of her busy evening care. She walked fast and purposefully, her mind on her patients.

That's not who I see now.

Before the accident, Trevor and I would sometimes run into each other in the hospital cafeteria. He would sit for a moment to say a quick hello and steal some food off my plate. What time will you be home today? I'd ask. I'm on call tonight, he'd tell me, his blue plastic beeper peeking out of a pocket. We would leave the cafeteria together and part with a hand squeeze, a quick hug. See you later.

Tonight the hospital corridor stretches empty and quiet behind us. Dr. Lewis has suggested the possibility of a nerve transplant from Trevor's leg to his face. If that worked, Trevor would be able to close his right eyelids and raise the corner of his mouth in a smile.

"The nerve graft idea sounds promising," I say.

Trevor doesn't answer.

"Trevor? Don't you think so? Then you could kiss again." I am teasing, and for a moment the expression in his good eye smiles back.

"At first I didn't know how I would ever stand looking at you again, how I would keep loving you," he says hesitantly. I am stunned, frozen. His arm tightens around my waist. "You look so much better now. But we're not the same anymore, Trish."

"No."

"And we never will be."

In front of the elevators, Trevor wraps his long arms around me, pulling me close. I dig my fingers into the pile of his jacket and bury my head in its softness. We stand alone under the bright fluorescent lights, rocking slightly.

❧

Trevor's surgery went well. He must work daily now to open his seized-up jaw by inserting popsicle sticks between his upper and lower teeth. He has bounced back and is active and sociable with others, but he's quiet and uncommunicative with me. Our townhouse echoes with old ghosts, and we tiptoe around each other awkwardly. It isn't the home we left to go on a weekend backpacking trip three months ago; all that was familiar feels so foreign.

We go to Trevor's mother and stepfather's place for Christmas, welcoming the warmth and activity of a full house. Sarah and Jac live an hour's drive from Calgary, in Canmore, just inside the front ranges of the Rocky Mountains. Outside the living-room windows pine trees tower, their dark branches covered in snow. The mountains rise massively grey behind them and the sky stretches above, a cloudless blue. I stare out at this tranquil winter world.

It used to be that a trip to the Canmore house meant sitting and knitting, curled in one of the soft living-room chairs, pausing to eat fresh-from-the-oven cinnamon buns. Canmore was walks along the river dike with Sarah and Jac's big dog, Celyn, symphony music from the stereo, and good suppers around the family table with brothers and sisters, spouses and friends who had dropped by. It was a weekend to let go, sitting with Trevor in the evening, he back from a climb, warm and held and laughter shared. Peaceful Canmore house. Then, back to work and school, our blue Rabbit carrying us east to the city.

I am sitting in one of those soft armchairs now, my knitting ignored in my lap. I look through the glass at the trees and the mountains and wait. I am waiting for the brown furred bulk of a bear to come into sight. Would the glass be thick enough to stop the bear's charge? I doubt it. The trees are perfectly still. There is no wind. There is no bear yet. But still I sit vigilant.

"There is nothing out there!" My voice is loud in the silent house and full of impatience. "Stop it. Stop looking!"

Should I try to read something? No. I can't concentrate. I will lie down on the couch and wait for Trevor and the others to come back. They went out for a walk in the woods, and I was too fearful to go along.

A reporter from the *Calgary Herald* came to interview us a few days ago. I was nervous, and I gave him information I shouldn't have. The paper, with its headline "Horrifying Memories Healed by Time," lies in front of me on the glass-topped coffee table. The reporter has made the front page again with our story. This time it isn't too bad. But I am livid about one part. The reporter says Trevor and I look better than two people have a right to look less than four months after tangling with an angry grizzly bear. Better than we have a *right* to look? What kind of a statement is that? After the hours and hours in surgery, the months in hospital, we have every right to look as "well" as we do. I don't want to feel that I am disappointing as a bear-mauling victim. I won't give any more interviews. They just don't understand.

Across the room is the tall Christmas tree, decorated with iced cookies and bulbs and lights. It's pretty with its glow and reflected colours. There are presents under it, stacked in bright piles. I love Christmas. I'm glad Trevor and I are both alive and here for it, with family, all together. I didn't know what to get him as a present this year, and I couldn't tell him what to get for me. All I want is to sit with him and hold his big warm hand, to feel his scratchy beard against my face and hear him singing.

I lie wide-eyed and alert with the house very still around me.

Supper smells from the oven blend with the scent of Christmas tree. Paff the cat nudges at my hand with her tiny wet nose. She jumps onto my stomach, then settles into a furry circle and purrs with my petting. Warm there. She closes her eyes and places paw on nose. Her purring vibrates as she snuggles in. Cat weight and warmth and endless purring make me sleepy. I relax, safe for now.

❧

I'm alone in our townhouse in Calgary. I am restless. I put James Taylor on to keep me company, but then want quiet. I sit at my typewriter and gaze at the African violets flowering on the windowsill.

I have trouble seeing the typewriter print, with my right eye tearing. Angry, I mop it over and over again with a tissue. Trevor says I will destroy the skin around that eye if I continue to mop with such a vengeance.

I've registered in some non-credit courses at the university, one on self-esteem and another on creative writing. I'm too anxious to go back to work yet. My confidence is at an all-time low. These classes will get me out into the real world without the stress and pressures of functioning as a nurse.

Everyone tells me that I'm looking great, that I'm coping well. Why don't I feel it? I grieve for my eye. I will never look like I did before, never see like I did before, never have a full head of hair. I'm alive, yes. I have Trevor still. I didn't lose any limbs. I'm not starving. There isn't a war going on around me. There are lots of reasons to be grateful. I should make the most of the time I have, but I feel so unsettled. There are too many hours in a day. I only have to look in the mirror or rub my chin or go out and have people stare at me to be tormented by horrific images of being pinned down by the bear, her mouth on my head, crunching.

There was a stage of "Oh my God" from ourselves and everybody else. There was a stage of shock and pity and disbelief. What is *this* stage called? I still feel sorry for myself, but I'm impatient to get on with things. I want to tell everyone how awful it was and shock them, and have them tell me how brave and wonderful I am. Yet I also don't want pity or people asking and talking about it all the time. And I still wish everything could be the way it used to be.

It's good to cry. It's good to sleep. But when I wake up, my sadness is still there.

❦

The counsellor's office is neutral, browns and rusts and beiges. I am always pleased to see Kathy's welcoming face.

"One minute I'm happy and positive, and then crash, the next moment I'm crying," I tell her. "I am so glad I can come here to vent and have my feelings accepted. It's all too much for Trevor and my mother and sisters."

Last week Trevor came to my appointment with me. He sat in silence as we drove there, disgruntled with my continuing nightmares, my refusal of a cross-country ski weekend, the amount of time I spend at the typewriter writing about the attack. At Kathy's, we sat at opposite ends of a long couch, describing the painful distance between us, talking to each other through her. Trevor said we were lucky to be alive. I don't want him to look crooked, I said, and I want my scars gone. He can't stand my fears and apprehensions, is sick of my need to rehash events. I protested that he has no patience, even complaining that I vomited too loudly after my last surgery. Life is good, he said. Let's just get on with it.

On the way home, we were silent again, but he took my hand and squeezed it when I reached across the gearshift to find his.

❧

On a stormy Sunday afternoon, I sit in a corner of our couch, knitting. Trevor is busy, pounding down the basement stairs and back up again carrying a pile of climbing gear, sorting through texts and papers spread all over the dining-room table, going in and out of the kitchen where he is making a pot of soup.

"Would you come and sit with me?" I ask. He looks at me,

surprised, stopping for a moment between kitchen and table to think. He bundles the climbing gear and piles it beside the couch, turns down the music, and sits. I continue to knit. He bends over his gear, checking and sorting.

"Don't you ever dream about it?" My voice and question startle us both. The words tumble out. "I mean, about what I looked like. Doesn't it bother you?" The need to talk is desperate within me. I look at him, fearing his disapproval.

After a pause, he responds. "I can't remember. I don't think about it." He is silent a moment. "I know I saw you, but really, I just don't remember."

"But it must have been awful. Weren't you afraid when you saw the bear?"

"All I saw was a brown flash to the side. I had a second to turn away and then she was on me." His fingers move down the slings, testing the knots. "I felt surprised. That's all."

"I saw her coming at you and coming up the tree and pacing afterward. It was *terrifying*. How could you only feel surprise?" He keeps his head down, sorting. I persist. "I didn't know she attacked you twice until we talked with Steve that day in the hospital."

"She got me by the leg the first time and pulled me down. When she left me it was to get you, but I didn't know that. I lay and waited and I heard two screams. The second one was cut off. I thought you were dead." At this, he pauses, searching my face.

"Then it was all quiet and I tried to get up and climb a tree and she came back at me from behind."

Dropping my knitting, I bring up my knees, hugging them. "Why didn't you hold still? Why did you get up?" My voice is plaintive. I struggle to shove away the image of the bear on him.

"I couldn't hear her moving around, and I thought she was gone. My ears were full of blood. I'd taken off my pack, and then she got me by the back of the neck and threw me back and forth. She hurt me the most that time. I was sure she would kill me. I felt curious. 'So this is how I die,' I thought."

I yearn to move close to him. I want to yell, "No!" I want to plug my ears and not hear any more. Tears threaten, but I don't want to frighten him away. He stares at me, unfocussed. Then I am angry.

"How could you feel so calm about death? I was petrified." My voice is urgent. "Didn't you think how upset I'd be? How could you not care about that?"

"But I thought you were already dead. Remember? I thought you were gone." He gets up to stir the soup, and I'm afraid he won't come back. But he does. He comes to my end of the couch, sitting close beside me and placing one arm over my shoulder. The house is quiet. Outside, a car engine starts up.

"What about the walk out?" I ask. "I was so afraid the bear would return. The other hikers, Jim and Joel, were shouting, 'No, no,' and I thought we would be attacked again. Even talking about it, my heart starts to beat faster."

"We won't be attacked again, Trish. We're predisastered." Trevor looks down at me and gains a wan smile. "I was focussed on surviving," he says. "I was thinking about hypothermia and blood loss and getting to the boat on time."

"At least I don't remember much pain."

His arm pulls me to him, fiercely. "Oh, Trish! You were in so *much* pain." He brings one hand up to the side of my face. The silence is long.

"Do you want to stop?" I ask.

"No. We need to do this."

"I want them to put it in books and brochures about twisting the bear's nose. It worked. She was treating me like dessert. It made her leave."

"You were always worried about bears. I wasn't. It wasn't going to happen to me."

"Trevor?" I am hesitant. "What about your face? Doesn't that bother you?"

"Mostly, I'm glad to be alive," he says. "My beard hides the worst of it. My nose can be fixed someday. It must be harder for you. Your patch and scars are so obvious."

"Yeah. And for men scars are more acceptable." For men it is macho to be scarred, I think, but society pushes a beautiful, unblemished face as the ultimate goal for women. Then I am uncomfortable, conscious of wanting it acknowledged that things are worse for me. Trevor plays along.

"You're left with a disfigurement that is right up front. People will notice it and ask what happened for the rest of your life."

I stiffen, remembering the time he told me he wasn't sure he'd be able to stand looking at me. I'm afraid he will say it again. I am hungry to hear that he loves me the way I am now, that the scars don't matter, but he is silent. For my part, I can't tell him of the distaste I fight, seeing his face. I don't want to hurt his feelings.

"Your eye is such a big loss, and the hospital was tough for you." He has pulled away to handle his climbing rack again. "You had so many long surgeries and such a lot of pain."

"Yes, and I have to have so many more surgeries. It's hard to yo-yo between being sick and being well, to be knocked flat by operations." He is gathering up his gear. "Trevor? Why don't you ever have bad dreams?"

His answer is clipped. "I did. I do." Then he bundles up the slings and carabiners and rope and is gone, clumping down the stairs to the basement again. I want to go after him, to apologize for bringing it up, for insisting we hike that weekend, for being the one to choose Crypt Lake Trail . . . Yet there is a tremendous relief in having spoken.

I get up to stir the soup, then sit with my knitting, alone again at the end of the couch. I know I'm not supposed to compare like I did, but it made me feel better. The knot in my stomach slowly comes undone.

The air is delicious, the sky blue and cloudless. There's not much snow on the ground, because we've had a lengthy February chinook. Pulling up in front of Erin's house, I feel good. Erin comes running down the stairs of her wide front porch to greet me. She's the wife of one of Trevor's classmates, and we've been friends for several years.

"Isn't it wonderful?" she exclaims. "Spring soon."

I unfold myself out of the Rabbit. "It's almost got the crispness of autumn to the air."

"How are you? I haven't seen you since that last surgery. What did they do? How did it go?"

"It wasn't bad. Just some adjustments to my left-eye mess. The graft on that eye is softening enough that I can move it a tiny bit by raising my eyebrow, and close it a bit by biting down. That's what's supposed to happen. So, progress."

Erin's arm comes over my shoulder. "Want to walk by the river?" she asks.

"Yes. Sure."

We walk the few blocks to the edge of the Elbow River, where a path runs for miles. Hands in our pockets, blowing our breath back into the cold air, we start to stride forward. I slow Erin down.

"I'm still not back in shape," I tell her, with a small laugh.

"What about Trevor? He had that big nerve graft surgery not too long ago. How's he doing?"

"It went well. But it was nerve-racking, no pun intended. Twelve hours of anesthetic. Sarah and I went shopping at Mount Royal Village. She called it tension relief, but I spent two hundred dollars! She did too." Erin's dark eyes sparkle. "Trevor's already felt some little movements on the grafted side of his face. The doctor calls them fasciculations. Someday he might be able to smile straight and kiss again."

She laughs, loud and long. "Oh, Trish. You have such a great attitude."

"You want to hear a rundown on me?" She nods. "Almost all of my lips move now and have sensation, even if it's a pins-and-needles feeling. The left side of my forehead feels gritty, but hey, it feels something. And the scalp graft: zaps and zows. It's called dysaesthesia when the nerves have been damaged and cause strange sensations."

Erin squeezes my arm tight to her side. "You're doing great," she says. "Are you still taking classes?"

"Yes. Writing is my favourite one." I look sideways and say tentatively, "I'm writing about the attack. It helps to get it out on paper."

"But you're over it, aren't you?"

"I can look in the mirror now and say to myself, 'That's me.' But I get sad if I look at pictures from before, especially the ones we took just minutes before it happened."

"Those pictures are still you." Erin's voice is earnest.

"I'm not the person in those pictures anymore. Not only

because my face has changed and my head's all scarred. My mind's done so many circles. It seems so long ago that that Patricia existed."

"But you've got so much going for you. And when you see all the patients dying of cancer, at least you're alive."

I rage inside. Why does it always come back to that? Of course, I'm glad to be alive. But why can't I be honest about the serious side of all this without people wanting me to be Joe Optimistic? But I play the game too, I think ruefully. Like now.

I force gaiety into my voice. "It's the start of a new life for me. I'm glad that our injuries weren't worse. I do feel lucky."

We turn homeward on the path. The sun glints on the slow, swirling eddies in the river. A woman with a baby carriage passes by.

"Blue skies and new babies make me happy again."

Erin leans into me conspiratorially. "Any new babies on the horizon for you and Trevor?"

"I'd love that, but we'll wait till things are a little smoother. We've got names picked out, though. We have had for years."

"What about an internship for Trevor? How's that going to work?" We are back in front of her house again. She asks me in for a cup of coffee, but I turn her down. I don't want her to know how tired I am.

"Trevor has missed six months of school. He'll graduate with next year's class."

I get into the car. Erin reaches in to hug me. "Are you guys going to come on the bike trip this spring? Up the Jasper highway?"

"I don't know. I'd like to." I say that, but I'm not sure what I feel.

"See you at the party at Don's tonight."

"Yes. See you there." As I drive away, I wonder how I can manage a party tonight. My mouth is tired from smiling and smiling.

I lie on the couch in our townhouse, staring up at the water-colour of Cascade Mountain given to us as a wedding gift. My feet cross and uncross as I try to get comfortable.

Trevor and I did go to the party last night. Medical students and their partners, dressed in corduroys and rugby shirts and wool sweaters, milled around the food table in little groups. I felt out of place in my floral skirt and turtleneck. I had replaced the wig I sometimes wear with a light pink kerchief.

People greeted Trevor and me enthusiastically as we moved through the room together. We stopped to talk here and there. There was the inevitable "You look great" and "God, you look good." Trevor and I held hands most of the evening, propping each other up, helping each other answer questions. Anna, one of Trevor's classmates, told me she saw me as a pretty person wearing an eye patch and didn't notice the scarring. That pleased me enormously. I don't know what to think about how I look. When I'm out in public, total strangers will say, "Wow. What happened to you?" Store personnel lean forward, raising their voices and articulating slowly, as if I am mentally handicapped. Yet the people who know me tell me I look wonderful. It's a crazy paradox.

Trevor comes in the front door to our tiny vestibule, where he peels off his bright yellow jacket and disintegrating leather shoes. He walks to the couch and laughs at my shrieks as he tucks his cold hands on my neck. We are closer after a few visits with Kathy. He pulls the brown and beige afghan my sister Margaret knit up over me.

"Hello, love."

"Hello, mister."

"I've been crusty, haven't I?"

"Yes. You have. And I'm up and down, all over the map."

"Wasn't that party exhausting?"

"I was just thinking about it. It was nice to talk to people, but their politeness can be so aggravating, especially in response to our looks. I do feel a certain degree of happiness at seeing myself in the mirror now, though."

"Careful. Don't get carried away."

I poke him in the ribs. "It's just that I look better than I thought I ever would. I look acceptable. Don't I?"

"Acceptable! You're more than acceptable, you goof."

"Half of my face is me now. I feel good about that. Even lucky." For the moment, I mean it.

"Right. Torn apart by a bear, put back together with multiple surgeries. That sounds like one lucky lady, all right!"

"Oh, you know what I mean. After all, it could have been worse."

"What's that I hear you saying? It could have been worse? That's my line, not yours. Burns. Gunshots. Car accidents. Remember? We could be totally scarred, blinded, half-dead." He pulls back in mock horror.

"We still have lots of the old us to work with. Do you know what I mean?" He leans to embrace me, and I take his full weight across my chest. My hand goes up to hold the curls at the back of his head. "Some people are left with nothing. If someone had tried to talk me into feeling like this a month ago, I would have been tempted to punch them. But now I actually feel a little bit lucky."

"About time." His sarcastic voice is muffled in my sweater.

"It *comes* with time."

"Let's see how long it lasts."

❧

I almost skip as I leave the house today. Spring! The grass is still brown, and the north wall of our little entryway has small remnants of dirty snow. But the air is clean and crisp and fresh, and the sun is full of warmth. Bare tree branches are silhouetted against a sky so blue and high it fills me with exhilaration.

I'm going to take a long walk, ending up at the local mall for errands. I seem to have boundless energy, and I revel in the experience. I wave to our neighbour Rosemary through her living-room window. Out through the parking lot I go and onto the flattened grassy verge beside busy 40th Avenue, singing "Yellow Bird" under my breath.

My jeans are a white pair I've had for years. They'd gotten too tight, but they're loose now, and I've cinched them tightly with a beaded Banff belt. My sweater is thick grey and white and pink Lopi wool. Trevor's mom, Sarah, knit it for me last year. Trevor has one, too. The pink kerchief is knotted at the back of my neck, ends tucked in tightly to keep my head covered. The grafted area is numb if I touch it, yet it's sensitive to the coolness of the wind. I pull my shoulders square as I march alongside the endless traffic.

The mall is a monstrous complex with a massive parking lot. I know I could get overwhelmed quickly by all the goods and people and noise, so I'll just pick up some eye patches at the department store and rummage in the fabric department for material for some new head scarves. I close my eye for a moment to stand and soak up the sun before going inside.

The lights in the store are bright. Displays of jewellery, scarves and purses slow my step as I browse. The scarves are gorgeous, but too silky, too large, too flamboyant for me. Sarah wants me to dress myself up more. She suggested I make eye patches to match my outfits. "Be proud of your experience and your scars," she urged me yesterday. "Your patch is your badge of courage. Flaunt it!"

Thinking of her words, I decide to try on some scarves. What the heck? I'll have to bare the back of my head to do it, but I'll just ignore the stares.

I search out a saleswoman to ask for a mirror. I see one up the aisle and lean my head with a smile to catch her eye. The woman looks at me, and her face stiffens. I stop, then glance over my shoulder to see what she's reacting to. Nothing. Just me. I raise my chin, continuing along the aisle. She is suddenly very busy with something on the counter in front of her. I draw closer, and just as I am ready to say "Excuse me," she turns on her heel and hurries away to a nearby cash desk.

I should pursue her. Make her deal with me. A small surge of anger presses through me, and I take a few steps towards the cash desk. But there are too many people there, staff and customers in lineups. I am suddenly flattened. The lights and the noise threaten to crush me. I want to go home.

The eye patches are in the pharmacy department on the other side of the store. I wend my way through the menswear department to avoid the people in the central aisles. There are only two boxes of patches on the shelf, and I grab them both. I know I should be buying in bulk to get a lower price, but it's as though I still think one day I won't need them anymore.

The clerk at the cash register stares openly, then smiles.

"Looks like you've been in the wars." His accent is British.

I smile my little smile back. "I had a bad accident."

"Really? What happened? A car crash, like?"

A quick debate inside me. Do I tell him the truth? I have no energy for telling the whole story today.

"It was a crash. I'm all right."

"Scratched your eye, did you? Going to be fine, though, I suppose?"

"Yes, I'll be fine."

Oh, you're so gracious, I think to myself. So pleasant. So helpful. Such a chicken.

"Well, have a good day. Watch out for cars, won't you?" He laughs at his little joke.

I let the wind that's come up blow me home. The sun is gone, and the clouds that have gathered are leaden. The wind wrestles with my scarf, creeping in and chilling the back of my head.

In the courtyard of our townhouse, the neighbourhood children are at play. There is a group of about nine of them, some very tiny, a few school age. Two older girls twine around a small sapling, teasing each other and giggling. They stop as I approach.

"Are you the lady that got attacked by the bear?" asks the dark-haired one.

The children turn towards me.

"Yes, that's me." I try to appear friendly and warm. I am acutely conscious of eighteen eyes examining me, and of the staring windows of the other houses around the courtyard.

"Did the bear do that to your eye?" the second little girl asks.

"Yes." I sigh, resigning myself. These kids live here and will see me all the time. I might as well give them the story. Maybe they'll take it home and tell their families, and then fewer people will ask about it. "The bear hurt my eye quite badly. It doesn't look very good anymore, and I wear this patch to cover it up."

"How did the bear get you?" asks a boy.

"Well, she ran very fast. She was eating and we got too close and she got angry with us. Usually bears just run away, though. Usually."

The first girl pipes up again. "My mom says you have to have an operation. Will that fix your eye?"

"I have had six operations already," I tell her, "They'll do some more, but they can't fix my eye. It got hurt too badly."

They are quiet. The littlest ones have gone back to filling and emptying buckets of sand.

"I'm going home now. I'm cold," I say, turning away. "Bye."

"Bye," they chant in unison.

Inside the house, I head straight for the bedroom. Supper needs preparing, but it can wait. I throw myself on the bed and tear off my kerchief, burying my face in the pillow. I lie there expecting to cry, but there is only a great emptiness. I rock myself back and forth, back and forth. Trevor will be home soon, and I want to get out of this mood before he arrives.

❦

Trevor and I are going on a hike with his anatomy professor, Paul, and his wife, Dana. It is a cool cloudy Saturday in May, and they laugh at me in my puffy down jacket, telling me I'll be taking it off in no time. I am glad to be here but apprehensive. Last weekend Trevor and I went for a fifteen-minute walk up Heart Creek. I had to turn around, I felt so sick. That night I had horrible nightmares, sensations of falling, accompanied by a crushing sense of doom. But it was snowing that day in the mountains, and today it isn't.

Trevor stands beside the car, pulling on his pack. I crouch to retie my boots. Paul and Dana get out most weekends to hike or ski in the mountains. McConnell Ridge, the hike they've chosen today, is through open aspen parkland on golden, trampled-looking grasses. The snow-topped mountains rise all around us. The evergreens are hundreds of yards away, yet I catch myself scanning, scanning.

When I stand to mingle with the others, Dana links her arm through mine. "I'll be okay," I tell her, my voice level and measured. I'm going to do my best at this. Defy the fear. Dare the bears. Please Trevor with my efforts. We begin walking, our boots crunching on the loose gravel, and Trevor comes to my other side. "Hey, you guys. I'm okay, I said."

"We just like you, that's all." Trevor squeezes my hand, his eyes focussed on the peaks around us. He points out one that he has climbed and details his route.

"I don't think there's much of a bear problem around here. Not that I've heard of," Paul says, looking at me.

"Down at the townsite, that's different. Plenty of bears. But they're garbage bears there. They end up killing them or shipping them out," Dana adds.

"But there's really no point in shipping them out," I cut in. "Even hundreds of miles away, they know where to come back to. They don't get lost, even though they are drugged for the trip. A kind of sixth sense, I guess." I have done a great deal of reading on bears' habits since the attack, devouring stories of other maulings, trying to get a perspective on our own.

Trevor stops and turns in a circle. "It's like being in a bowl. We're just off the bottom of it. See?" We all turn and look. "Trish, can you imagine this place if there were no bears?"

"I'd love it. Sometimes I wish there were no bears anywhere. But they are such amazing animals," I add, wanting to say the correct thing. But I am not convinced.

Dana pulls open her pack to get a drink. "Maybe one day you'll visit the Southern Alps in New Zealand, where there are no predators."

"I know lots of people say the bears belong here, and they were here first," I continue. "Sometimes I understand that. And it's worse to be a bear. They are far more likely to be killed by humans than humans are to be killed by them."

"Let's just hike," Trevor says.

Approaching the car at the end of our walk, I have to stop

myself from running. I can't wait to get inside. Out of the cold and away from the constant vigilance. I sit quietly in the back, Trevor's hand in both of mine, anxious to get home. Back to my bed, under the big comforter. And safety.

❧

Our big picture window looks out on other brick and cedar student-housing units. The sky is cloudy today. The trees have tiny buds, and the ground is dotted with patches of new grass. It has been nine months since our accident.

This is home, and I like being here. I have finished vacuuming, doing the dishes and putting supper to warm in the oven. The oval rug I crocheted stretches along the floor in front of the couch. Bright pillows are scattered in the old armchair of my parents' that we reupholstered. Our Coke-crate footstool has Trevor's fat medical textbooks open on it. I sit alone in the silence, thinking.

Last week we invited Jim and Joel for dinner, the two hikers who came along after our attack. They were shy and quiet during an awkward evening. They told us they had stopped to take pictures up on the ridge; if they hadn't, they would have walked right in on the attack. Both of them still have nightmares. They had received an award for bravery, they said. Without their help, we would not have survived.

Trevor and I know now that the weather that day helped to

save us. Because of the cold we were wearing bulky layers of clothing, which protected us from more severe body lacerations and puncture wounds. Without the three inches of snow my head lay in, I would have bled to death, no matter how determined I was to live. The snow and cold air constricted our blood vessels enough to prevent our bleeding to death during the almost three-mile hike out of the area.

We wouldn't have survived the freezing six-hour wait for the next lake shuttle if Trevor had not gone on ahead, either. He ran the last mile of the trail to catch the boat on time, holding his face together with one hand and his damaged leg with the other. He emerged from the trees just as the boat was completing its last circle of the bay.

Looking at the evergreens outside our window, I shiver. Though my will to live was strong, I know it wasn't enough. It's almost as if someone up there didn't mean for that attack to be the end of us. How did I fall twenty feet from the tree and avoid breaking any limbs? How did the bear manage to maul Trevor and expose the critical carotid artery, tearing away its surrounding tissues, yet leaving the artery intact? The surgeon told us it was the most perfect dissection of an artery he had ever seen. Trevor's thigh was also torn open, just half an inch from the femoral artery. Had either of these vessels been severed, he would have died within moments.

I stretch and yawn in the late afternoon sun's dim warmth, staring vacantly ahead of me.

I can wish it never happened, but it did. I will cry about it and feel sorry for myself. I will cry for Trevor and the distortion his face now wears. I will cry over the changes in our relationship. And I will be angry that I can never feel the same way about hiking in the Rockies, grieve the loss of that shared love.

I want to feel proud of how far I have come, of doing things my way. I will read about grief and body image and bears until I don't want to delve anymore. People can tell me to stop dwelling on it, to get on with my life, but I *am* getting on with my life. They can tell me the attack is in the past, but it isn't. I will deal with it every day for the rest of my life. I look around at the home Trevor and I have put together. I admire us for being here and coping as we do.

I can see Trevor through the window, carrying our four-year-old neighbour, Jason, around the lawn on his shoulders. It's good to see him laughing after a long night on call and a full school day. We're back to the same old grind, soon to be complicated with my schedule of nursing. I'm starving. I'll go and call Trevor in. Supper and a hug.

IV

Falling

It is over a year since our accident, and I am back at work, part-time, on the orthopedics floor. My patients here have broken bones. My other choice was ophthalmology, but I couldn't imagine being an eye-patched nurse on a ward where most of the patients wear eye patches, too. In orthopedics there is more heavy lifting, but the patients stay longer, and I like the chance to get to know them.

I'm excited about my new job but nervous, too. I'm still so thin that my old uniforms fit loosely. My face has filled out some, and the scars have faded enough to be less visible. My right eye is bright and blue. There will be no new surgeries for me until early spring at least. My scars need more time to soften and heal.

At first I am self-conscious as I move through the rooms making my rounds. I check vital signs, test for warmth and sensation in hands or feet at the ends of casts. Many of my patients are immobilized by traction, with one or two limbs suspended. The shiny metal pins that connect them to the silver machinery are sometimes drilled right through the bone. I clean the pin sites and once in a while rewrap a limb supported in a sling with sterile gauze.

Very quickly, I learn that the patients don't notice anything strange about my appearance. Their visitors, however, often challenge me, as if afraid my disfigurement has affected my competence. One patient's father squints in my direction, then reaches up to cover one eye, something small children often do when they see me. "You can see?" he asks gruffly. "Are you really a nurse?"

"Yes, I'm a nurse. And I see just fine. I only have one eye to see from, but it works." I smile at him. He returns my look, unsmiling.

Rick, in 325, is only seventeen. He was driving a car in an accident that killed two people. The other nurses have warned me about him, told me to watch out for swear words and flying food. I speak as I approach his bed. No answer. His good arm looks skinny where he has flung it over his eyes. I stand at the side of the bed, noticing his unfinished food tray. I try again. "You're not hungry today? The other nurses tell me you're not eating." His hair is short and spiky, and freckles spread thickly across his forehead and cheeks. He doesn't speak, but I notice his chin is trembling. He is crying.

"Rick, my name's Trish. I'll be your nurse for a while. What's up?" I lean quietly into the bed.

"Go away." He tries to shift away from me, but with both legs in traction, he can't.

"I'll go now, but I have to come back later to rewrap your hand and dress your screw sites. I'd like to talk with you."

"Go away."

Outside his room, I stop one of the other nurses. "Isn't Rick from somewhere in northern Alberta?"

"Yes," she answers. "Camrose. Was he being difficult? I hear he's got quite the temper."

"He's only a kid. Isn't there any way he could be closer to his family? Edmonton?"

She sighs, turning away. "If he keeps up his acting out, maybe they'll send him packing."

"Maybe he could go home *before* it's too big a problem," I mutter to myself. He needs more help than he's getting here.

On my night shifts, I often sit with patients through the dark and difficult hours. I am spending more time with patients than before my accident, trying to listen to their feelings and needs. By caring for them in this way, I am meeting a deep need in myself. But doing so forms a rift between me and the other nurses, who sit at the desk reading magazines and talking. They have nicknamed me the PSBS nurse, for PsychoSocial BullShit. I don't care. Rita, in 340, has a fractured pelvis and can't move. She's the mother of three young children, and she's worried about how her husband is coping. If I can spend forty-five minutes listening to her and letting her cry, she's often able to sleep for a few hours afterward.

Rick cries a lot at night, but he tries to hide it. I've taken to standing at his bedside and talking quietly to him. Usually he listens without answering. Occasionally he tells me to leave. "I know you don't think anything can help, Rick. But this is such a big deal. You were the driver of the car. You've got broken legs and a broken arm and you're in a lot of pain."

I have never seen his eyes. He always covers them with his gauze-wrapped arm. I lean against the bed, not touching him, and tell him my story. Not the details of the attack, but about the injuries and surgeries, the endless nights, the atrocious nightmares.

"Do you have nightmares too?" No answer. No movement.

One morning when I am working day shift, there is a crash from Rick's room. I go to check it out. The nurse is angrily picking up food from the floor and telling Rick off.

I finish my own work, then return. Rick is motionless on his bed as usual, his eyes covered, his jaw set and fierce. "You know, someday maybe we could take you outside. Just for a change of scenery. Would you like to try that?"

I look around the room. On the wall over his bed, some small child's drawings are pinned up.

"Where did the pictures come from?" I ask. "Who did them?"

Rick convulses in tears abruptly. He tries to roll the top half of his body away from me, then gives up, and his good arm comes down to grab at my hand. I lean towards him. He chokes out the words. "They're from my little brother."

"How old is he?"

Through sobs, he answers. "He's five. His name is Robbie. I hate it here. I want to go home."

"Just cry," I whisper.

"They don't have the money to come and see me. I just want to go home."

When his crying slows and his grasp relaxes a little, I speak. "I'll talk to the head nurse about getting you transferred. I don't have a lot of say in it, but I'll see what I can do."

The charge nurse tells me she'll check with the doctor. The nurses are quite fed up with Rick's behaviour. I ask her about getting a counsellor he could talk with. "I'll look into it," she says.

For the next three weeks I am off for one of my own surgeries. They take half a rib and place it in the left side of my face, where the cheekbone is missing. The donor site is painful, and when I return to work I am still protective of it.

The surgery sets me back. My emotions are all over the map again, and Trevor and I are irritable with each other. Trevor visited me in the hospital, but I could tell he didn't want to be there. It is difficult to straddle two worlds, to be the patient and the nurse. In two months I will go back for surgery again.

Rick is gone. They never did get anyone in to talk to him, and his behaviour deteriorated. Finally, they shipped him out to a hospital closer to his home. "I don't know where you got the patience for him, Trish," one nurse comments. I stand in the busy hustle of the desk, looking at the doctors and interns and nurses around me. I have the sudden urge to scream at them. It's so obvious that Rick needed to vent his anger and sadness, that he needed to be cared about and loved just as much as he needed the casts and the traction. Afraid of becoming further estranged from the other staff or sounding preachy, I hold my tongue.

❦

One night on rounds, I see a familiar name on the charts: Tom Braden. That's the name of one of the doctors at the hospital in Cardston, where we were first cared for after the attack. I wonder if this is the same guy. I never saw him; I just remember his name coming up.

I enter Tom Braden's room quietly, pushing the wide door out of my way. He is in multiple traction, I see as I approach the bed. I know from his chart that he has survived a car accident in which his pregnant wife was killed.

"Hi," I say. His eyes glow in the dim light. "Not able to sleep?"

"No."

"I'm Trish."

"I remember you. One of the other nurses told me you were here."

"So you *are* from Cardston." I move closer to the bed.

"Yes. Your accident was quite a big event in our community. How are you doing? Did your husband get back to work too?"

"Yes, he's finishing up his third year of med school. We've applied for residencies on the West Coast. But what about you? I'm so sorry to hear about your wife and baby. What a terrible blow. At least Trevor and I both survived."

"Ah well, you can't compare. It *is* hard. Very hard."

Orange street lights shine through the plaid curtains. I don't know what to say, so I reach for his hand. He holds on but looks away.

"You and your husband were in pretty rough shape. Did they get the bear?" He is fighting to hold back tears and wants to change the subject.

"They had to shoot the bear," I tell him.

"You've been through so much," Tom says. He hesitates. "Do you have nightmares?"

"Yes. And visions in the daytime that torment me. I'm frightened almost all the time. Afraid of driving, afraid of dogs, afraid of strangers. I don't trust the world at all."

After that, Tom and I visit almost every night. Sometimes he can sleep, but not often, and so we talk. The other nurses and I move in separate worlds. I can't relate to the conversations about shopping and holidays and dinner parties. I am so close to my own suffering and that of my patients that the daily activities of life seem mundane and irrelevant. Nothing but pain seems to have any meaning.

In May, I go for another surgery. Sitting up in my hospital bed, I talk with the anaesthetist, an older man who won't look at me and speaks in a monotone like a robot. I'm scared. The more anaesthetics and surgeries I have, the more apprehensive I become.

The operating room is green-tiled and cold as I am wheeled in. My body shakes with a fine tremor. I yearn for a word with my surgeon, but he doesn't come. His new resident, someone I've never seen before, comes instead. "You'll be fine," the resident bellows, clapping an enormous hand on my forearm.

My head hurts when I wake up, but the pain is not excruciating. They have made much of the incision through scalp area that is numb. A flattened balloon called a tissue expander has been placed under my scalp, on the top of my head where there is hair. It will remain there for six weeks. Each week I will visit the emergency department to have the balloon inflated a small amount. When it is fully inflated and I look like a conehead, they will remove the expander and pull the newly stretched skin down over the bald grafted area on the back of my head. Eventually, I will have a full head of hair.

By the time I return to work, the first two inflations have been done, and there's a raised bump on the top of my head showing through the kerchief. I am in constant pain. I feel something's wrong. But my doctor is short-tempered when I try to discuss it with him, so I try to ignore the discomfort.

Tom Braden has spent the long weeks in traction. We talk frequently about pain, about loss, about changes. We are existential together.

"Does it make you wonder why you're here?" he asks.

"Yes, and what I am supposed to be doing. If I died tomorrow, what difference would that make to the world? Where do people go when they die? Where are your wife and baby now?"

"Why did they die, and not me?"

I look out the window and sigh. "I wish Trevor would talk about these things with me. Why is he so shut down about it? Maybe he's right and I should just stop dwelling on all of this."

"How can you, when you're still living it?" Tom says. His words comfort me.

I am in my counsellor's office in tears. I have just been to emergency, for another inflation, and the pain is severe. There is a hard, hot area towards the back of the expander, and the inflation tube is exposed at a red and tender spot along the suture line. The doctor has prescribed antibiotics, but they're not helping. I sit with my head in my hands, telling Kathy that the pain is destroying me. Trevor has no patience for it, or for my other difficulties. We're hardly even talking to each other. I can't sleep, and so I've camped out on the couch. I can't handle work. I can't relate to the world. Can't feel safe. Can't be close to anyone. I feel so incredibly alone.

Kathy leans forward in her chair, staring fiercely at me with large, chocolate eyes. "Trish. Listen to me. Don't get sad. Get mad."

I still my body's rocking. Tears course down my right cheek.

"You've got to tell the doctor how much you hurt and refuse to leave his office until something is done to make you feel better. Go. Now."

I walk to my car in a daze. Use the anger, she said. I'm not very good at that. But I am angry, all right. I know that something is amiss. I am not imagining the constant pain.

The doctor's receptionist looks up in surprise when I enter the crowded waiting room. I tell her that I won't be leaving until I've seen someone. I plunk myself in a chair and lean my sore head back against the wall. A pulse beats loudly in my head. Without warning, warm fluid pours down my neck. The hard, hot area under the scalp has ruptured. Murky fluid runs down the white wall and onto the carpet.

The receptionist stares at me, speechless. The other patients are looking on, some with disgust.

I laugh for the first time in weeks. I feel better already.

❧

I lie back against the driftwood log and watch, one hand up to shield my eyes from the sun. Trevor fights with the enormous sail of his new windsurfer. The ocean waves toss him up and down as he tries to balance, a long, black eel-like figure in his wetsuit.

Trevor's internship choice in Victoria, British Columbia, was awarded, and we moved out to the coast fast enough for me to still feel surprised to find us here. It is summer, almost two years since our accident. Our new home is the second floor of a two-storey stucco cube. The windows are large, and when they are open, the ocean air blows straight through the few large rooms. We look out on a sea of treetops.

Trevor and I feel lighter here. We share a happy optimism about a new start where no one knows us as the bear attack victims. Vibrancy and good health course through us; we are close again, friends in this adventure.

One afternoon, I go to the hospital and look at the job board. I ask about part-time jobs at the personnel desk. A nurse standing beside me comments on my eye patch. I explain sharply, and she turns away.

At the hospital in Calgary, I was known and accepted. The head nurse who gave me the job on orthopedics knew me before the accident. If I applied for a job here, would they doubt my abilities? Could I be turned down because of my disfigurement? At dinner that night, I tell Trevor. "I chickened out."

"On what?"

"On applying for a job at the hospital."

"You don't have to work," he says.

"I need to do something. I'll go crazy sitting around here."

"What about your writing? You could do that."

The rice in the pot has gone hard, and I pound at it with a spoon.

"Take it easy on that rice. You'll mash it," he says gently.

"I don't want to do my writing here. I want to put it away for a while. I want to do something with other people. I want to feel normal. To merge."

"What about doing your nursing degree at the university here?"

"That's a wonderful idea!"

"Good. Pass the mashed rice, please."

The University of Victoria is beautiful. The grounds are arrangements of towering old trees, big flowering bushes and flower beds showing a profusion of colour. Shaded walkways crisscross wide-open green lawns.

The instructors and the other students welcome me without question. I organize my projects, wherever possible, around issues of facial disfigurement, writing papers on burn unit in-services and working with a patient at the hospital who lost his nose to cancer. Before long, I have new friends. We walk down the hill at lunch break to a little shopping plaza beside the ocean to eat pasta and salads while sitting on wrought-iron chairs in the sun. I go to Deirdre's huge old house in Oak Bay to groan and complain and laugh as we do our assignments together. I meet with Rose and her five-month-old son, drinking coffee in her immaculate kitchen as we compare notes on our doctor husbands and help each other prepare for exams.

One evening at home, I put my head back on our tall armchair. My biochemistry text is on my lap, waiting to be struggled through.

"Trevor?"

He is flipping through pictures of a decrepit sailboat he wants to buy. "Mmm?"

"I like it here. I'm glad we came."

He looks up in surprise. "You're happy?"

I smile with the pleasure of it. "Yes. I'm happy."

We are at a Christmas fair, walking the aisles slowly as many things compete for our attention. Some weavings catch my eye, and I pull Trevor over to look. He picks up a yellow baby blanket.

It is woven on one side, lined in yellow flannelette and patterned with tiny flowers. We hold it between us.

"Did you do all this work?" I ask the woman in the booth. I move my fingers over the weaving, which is dotted with minuscule embroidered pink-and-green rosebuds.

"Yes. So long it took me. I'm still not sure I want to sell that one."

I hold it to my face, then turn it over to feel the softness of the flannel.

"Would you sell it to us?" Trevor asks. We are holding on to the blanket as though we can't let go.

"Oh, all right," the woman says. "It looks like it will have a happy home. When are you expecting?"

"Oh! I'm not," I answer.

When we get home, I drape the quilt over the back of the couch and smile.

I am shaking with excitement as I drive to see Trevor at the hospital. He's in the cafeteria, they tell me. I spot his dark, curly head across the room, and he stands and waves as I walk to greet him. My face is splitting ear to ear in an enormous grin.

"Trevor. I have something to tell you."

"What?" His hand reaches to stroke my face. "You are so beautiful right now."

I hold out a single white rose. "This is for you, Daddy."

"Really, Trish? Really?" He holds me to him, lifting my feet off the ground, then hits the table beside him and whoops. The other interns at his table applaud. I sit in a cloud of bliss, thinking of the infant started within.

I lean towards Trevor and whisper. "I was pregnant when we bought the blanket."

He kisses me on the cheek, then pushes his food in front of me. "Eat, eat," he says.

For seven more months I eat. I swell to 170 pounds. People exclaim at how round I am. I waddle around, complaining of the heat. At the end of the school year, I pack my papers and assignments away. I will go back to school part-time when the baby is here, I tell myself, and get my degree that way. I assemble baby gear. The cradle Trevor built sits against the wall in one of our lovely, sunlit rooms. "There's room in there for triplets," Deirdre comments. "Might be," I agree.

I cry in the night sometimes. At first, I was terrified of a miscarriage. Later, I began to wonder if the baby would be all right. What if he or she is mentally handicapped like my sister Mary, who has spent half of her life in an institution? What if we have a baby with a cleft lip and palate, something visible and facial? Or what if the baby doesn't take to me, with a face that's out-of-balance? By the end of the pregnancy, I am worrying about the delivery. Will this baby live? Is it possible that things could go all right? I don't know what I believe about God these days, but nonetheless I pray. Will I be a good mother? Our lives will change so much. Some nights I dream I am falling from the tree, through endless black space, screaming and reaching out for something to grab hold of. The enormous weight and animal smell of the bear is right behind me, falling too. I never land, just fall and fall and fall into darkness, in terror of the bear catching up with me.

I feel gloriously feminine as well as heavy and cumbersome. The baby moves in large, sweeping motions, delighting me. Trevor holds his head against my abdomen talking to the baby and thrilling at the bumps and bulges. We are well into summer, and my parents have come here for the baby's birth. We have walked from our box-shaped old home to the ocean, just two blocks away, over and over again. The due date is long past. My mother and I hold hands, and I plague her with questions. Was Gordon, her first baby, overdue? Were any of us? How did she feel when Mary was born? Did she ever resent being the one at home with the kids? My father sits in our back yard in the shade, untangling a reel of fishing line. I offer to help him pick the black-berries growing rampant around the perimeter of the little yard, but he sends me away, his eyes crinkling as he squints into the sun. He does not want me to be scratched.

Trevor spends hours working on his new boat, an old wooden Thunderbird, tearing out orange shag carpet, reupholstering the seats, and enlisting my help in painting the cleaned-out insides a creamy white until my belly makes it difficult for me to get into the little cabin. We take the boat out often, mastering the rudiments of ocean sailing. Between trips I chafe with impatience, worry and discomfort. I lie in the still of night, Trevor asleep beside me, and rub my hands over and over the bump with life inside it.

A girl. Nicola Rose. She's big and healthy. I'm proud of myself for getting through the delivery. Proud of us for producing this amazingly gorgeous little person. My father cries, his love tangible and full holding Nicola's new perfection.

We wrap her in the wonderful yellow blanket and parade to the local tearoom, sure nobody else has ever felt this happy. Some days Trevor pops her into the Snugli and her bright, birdlike eyes peer over the edge at her new world. Sarah brings us a stroller, then opens her suitcase to show nighties and blankets and toys.

In the early September evenings, when the nights begin to cool, we sit with our Nicola on a sheepskin in front of the fire. She struggles to lift her big head and keep her eyes open, drowsy in the warmth. I stretch out on the carpet in total contentment, Trevor's body close beside me.

W hen Nicola is only four weeks old, Trevor gets a letter telling us that his residency, applied for a year ago, has been accepted. The placement is in Dunedin, New Zealand. Looking at pictures in library books, I thrill with the anticipation of exploring the country of green hills, sheep, beaches and mountains; a country without bears. We will be able to hike again, see a new culture, ramble in the shops and streets of unknown towns. But how can we leave the security of the people and places we are nurtured by when Nicola is so young, so new? This fear pulls at my heart.

In a frenzy of activity we hurry to store our belongings, pack what we need, get our passports in order. Our families encourage us. They will visit. We can phone. There will be letters. Finally, with a mixture of excitement and uncertainty, we walk the vast spaces of the airport, carrying our infant to the airplane that will transport us.

The apartment we are assigned in Dunedin has cavernous rooms. A love seat in the living room faces empty walls until Trevor purchases a battered piano that warms the room with its presence but will not stay in tune. Our few belongings hardly make a dent in the place. I put up magazine pictures to add colour. Nicola distracts and delights us, but Trevor and I are moody. He is challenged by irregular shifts and work that is unfamiliar and difficult. I am tired, up with Nicola in the night, alone with her all day, fighting pain that has developed in my face.

Steep, steep streets rise up from the ocean, forcing me to lean into the pram as I strain my way to the top. The air is cold, though it's summer here. My body is stiff, bundled in wool, as I make my way past brick houses to the clinic of the Plunkett nurses. They will assess Nicola and do her vaccinations. I tell the nurses, Mabel, Pauline and Bobbie, that I have been in Dunedin two months and I am lonely. Three sets of eyes focus on me, heads nodding in unison. They take the howling Nicola from her pram and motion me to an ancient armchair where I am served tea and bikkies. I talk nonstop, about missing my family and friends, about being alone so often. Trevor is working many twenty-four-hour shifts, and he goes rock climbing at the beach cliffs in his spare time. I've tried going with him, but it is difficult sitting for hours on the windswept sand with Nicola. I tell the nurses how tired I am, with the baby not sleeping at night. I ask them to recommend a doctor. I have such pain in my left eye these days.

The University of Dunedin is walking distance from our apartment, and I find I can take two psychology courses that I require for my degree. An enchanting daycare centre beside the university will take Nicola. The babies there are round and red-cheeked in their woollen leggings and "jumpers." Several half days a week I am free to cruise the shops in the small downtown, do my schoolwork or go home to take a nap, cradling the ache in my face and head.

Trevor and I make some friends, Robyn and Dave and their baby, Cara. Robyn is a vibrant redhead, a nurse who works part-time in the intensive care unit at the hospital where Trevor is working. Dave is a housedad. Robyn and Dave are also climbers, and they sub off with one another on our outings. When it's Robyn's turn to mind Cara, we walk together on the miles and miles of endless gold sand, peering up at our husbands on the rock face high above us.

Many weekends Trevor and I explore the hikes Robyn has told us about. Trevor carries our clothes and gear, and I carry Nicola in her backpack. The trails meander past streams and hill-sides in a landscape that resembles Canada until we hit forests thick with junglelike growth and the noise and movement of exotic birds. There are huts along the way, with rows of bunks and cooking facilities and the inevitable harassment of the kea bird, a brown parrot with a raucous cry and an insatiable desire to destroy camping gear. It is exhilarating to be high on a pass, with peaks all around, the air clear and crisp, and know that there are no spiders or snakes that could injure us. And no predators. No bears.

Robyn's spritely nature brings laughter to my life. She and Dave and Cara live in a rundown little cabin at the back of an old estate home. The doorway is low, just off the back alley. There is mess from one end of the place to the other. The low-ceilinged living room is hung with the laundry: Cara's nappies, Dave and Robyn's knickers and wool socks and undervests.

Robyn brings me coffee, yelling at Dave to give up the only upholstered chair. She tucks me into her bed one day when my face is swollen and throbbing, kicking a pathway to the bedroom through the debris. I can't sleep, but I rest, smelling the fresh line-dried linens on her bed and revelling in the love and companionship I've found.

But it is difficult between Trevor and me. I hardly ever see him, and I am crabby when I do. One night as we lie in bed, our backs to each other, I lash out.

"I feel like I can't be enough for you. I can't please you. You seem to think it's my job to make you happy. I can't help it if I'm not pretty anymore." I stop for a breath, then resume. "I can't be delighted to see you when you've been gone for two or three days and I haven't slept at night and my face is so sore."

"I don't sleep either. Remember that. I'm at the hospital."

"Nicola's a lot of work. It's lonely without you. I miss everyone so much. And I'm sick."

"When are you going to see that doctor?"

The tears begin gathering in my eye. "I don't want any more to do with doctors."

I feel Trevor's body heave upward. "Sit up," he says.

I sit beside him, my tears rising. He takes my chin in one hand and gently taps the left side of my face, percussing my sinuses for evidence of infection. "Trish, you're hot."

"No, I'm cold. I can never get warm in this country. Winter without central heating. I have to hover with my butt five inches above the toilet seat if I don't want frostbite." I sob.

"No, I think you've got a fever. I'll get some acetaminophen."

By the time he comes back, I have soaked both my pillow and his with tears.

"No wonder you don't want to go to the mountains with us this weekend. Maybe I should stay here with you." His voice is heavy.

"I'm not scared to go to the mountains, Trevor. I've gone with you all the other times. I love hiking here with no bears. But I'm just so tired. All I want to do is sleep."

"We'll get you some antibiotics." He lies back down beside me. "I'm sorry about my distance and the grumpiness. I don't know what's going on."

The doctor at the clinic prescribes antibiotics and a stronger painkiller. I wave good-bye to Trevor and Nicola, who head off for the mountains in a car stuffed with camping gear. With relief, I turn back to the silent apartment. Sleep.

Trevor's parents come to visit for Nicola's first birthday, and we drive together to a cabin on Lake Wanaka, in the middle of the South Island. The farmland and small towns along the way are colourful, but no one notices them much because Nicola will not stop crying. For hours and hours she howls. The car is small. Jac and Sarah's faces get longer and longer, till I hear Jac yelling to Sarah over the noise that they will take the bus on the return trip.

The cabin is spacious and bright. Nicola is learning to walk, and before we release her from the bedroom, Trevor and I rush around moving ashtrays and ornaments and standing lamps. That evening, we have a fire in the little gas fireplace, and Nicola falls asleep on Trevor's lap as he reads her *Goodnight Moon*. Her fair hair lies in curling wisps on his dark sweater.

The next morning Jac and Sarah shoo us out early. Trevor and I have planned a day away, just the two of us. He is in a black mood, and I can tell he doesn't look forward to the pleasure of my company.

We hike high up the edge of a hill overlooking the little town. "Couldn't we just try to have a good time?" I ask him.

"I don't want to talk."

I take the rejection inside and twist it around my heart. He doesn't love me. I'm disfigured and not skinny enough, not pretty and no fun. I walk on resolutely behind him.

At lunch I try again. "Why don't you order the burger and fries?" He doesn't even look up at me. "It was a joke." The burgers and fries here are fried in mutton fat. We almost gagged the first time we tasted them.

His smile is wan. He drapes one arm over my shoulder as we walk to the car. We are going to go horseback riding not far from the lake. It is my idea, a way to do something adventuresome with Trevor. I don't tell him, but the prospect fills me with fear. Horses are totally unpredictable animals to me. Thinking about their strong legs, their massive, tossing heads, and the height I will have to sit off the ground sets my heart pounding.

The ranch is small. "I don't see any horses," I say.

"There are a few on the side of that hill."

"They look too frisky."

"Are you afraid?"

I don't want to answer. I smile brightly.

Dale, the ranch hand, is crisp and no-nonsense. Yes, sure we can ride. Just a minute while she gets the horses. They're a little rambunctious. They've been out on the fells all winter. How experienced are we?

"Oh, we've got no experience. Something easy," Trevor says, placing his arm around my shoulder again. My stomach starts to churn.

The horses are all over the place when she brings them into a small corral. They throw their heads and whinny, tails whipping. I want to go and hide in the car.

"Could I have the most gentle one?" I ask.

"They're all pretty gentle, really, mate." She moves around, trying to saddle the energetic beasts. They look even bigger than I had imagined.

Dale helps me to mount. "Just make sure you let the horse know you're in control," she says.

She takes us through a few basics, and I try desperately to memorize what to do with the reins, the stirrups, my body. My heart is in my throat.

We start off, Dale in the lead. We get farther and farther from the farmhouse, and without warning Trevor's horse starts to wind up, first tossing her head, then taking little jumps, then bucking. Suddenly he is lying in the grass.

My heart is racing. Is Trevor's foot's caught in the stirrup? Is he moving? Is the horse going to step on him? Dale goes after the horse, which has calmed immediately to drop her head and eat grass twenty feet away. I want down. I fumble with the stirrups and reins, fighting back tears, shaking like a leaf, and eventually get myself to the ground.

Trevor is shaking his head ruefully and rubbing his hip.

"Are you okay, Trevor?"

"I'm fine."

"Let's go home."

Trevor rides Dale's horse back to the farmhouse, and she rides Trevor's naughty horse, leading mine. I walk.

✤

"Careful, Mommy," Nicola warns as we bring our groceries up the snowy front path to our 1960s bungalow. "It be slippy here." Last year, when we got back from New Zealand, Calgary was having full-blown winter. This year there is less snow, but it is bitterly cold.

"Nicola, you carry that little bag out to the kitchen. We'll get everything ready for our tea party. Are your children coming

too?" She smiles her pixie smile my way and races down the hall
to her bedroom. I am cutting the apple fritters into quarters
when she returns with her arms full. There are three bald baby
dolls, a small pink plastic high chair and two tiny bibs.

"All my babies will come. Auntie Gerry and Gramma want to
see them.

"Did you know Auntie Mary is coming too?"

"Is Auntie Mary the one who's got the hockey hat on her
head? Why does she?"

"Her brain doesn't work the same as ours. Sometimes she falls
down, and the helmet is so she doesn't hurt her head."

Half an hour later, the goodies are ready and the doorbell
rings. My sister Jane has picked up my mother, Mary and Auntie
Gerry, and she hustles them in out of the cold, carrying her one-
year-old, a stiff snowsuited bundle, under her arm. I pull my
mother aside as coats and boots and hats are wrestled to the front
hall closet.

"How were Dad's blood tests this week?" I ask my mother
hesitantly, wanting only good news. My father was diagnosed
with leukemia earlier this year.

"Fine. The treatment has helped, and the cell counts show
the leukemia is at bay for now."

I try to catch Mary's eye to say hello. She stares straight ahead
at a spot on the carpet, her arms held tightly at her sides. A smile
appears briefly when I give her a hug. She shuffles into the living

room, where she picks up a magazine and begins to turn each page carefully.

"How long is Mary home for?" I ask my mother.

"Just the weekend. They've changed her medication again."

"She seems so sedated." I look across the room. "Come on, Mary," I call. "We've got a tea party for you."

Auntie Gerry helps Mary get settled in her chair at the table, placing sandwiches on the plate, then sits down herself. "How is your face these days, Patricia?" she asks me.

"It's sore. I'm so tired of it. The operations help for a while, but they just don't last. I keep getting infections." I've had two sinus surgeries in the past eight months, and still the illness accumulates inside me, causing a constant, solid ache through the left side of my head. Everyone is quiet a moment. I hate to complain. Auntie Gerry herself is a trojan, never griping about her sore leg or chest pains. I glance at Mary's crooked nose, broken so many times from falling during seizures, and at the vacant expression her face wears. I smile brightly at everyone.

During the last few weeks, I have been isolating myself. I fight the cloak of bleakness and sadness that has wrapped itself around me. My favourite place to be is in bed, with the comforter pulled high around my ears, safe from a world of uncertainties. My family doesn't know how much I struggle.

I have an active and talkative two-year-old. I have a household to run, a husband who comes home each evening after shifts at a medical walk-in clinic. I have the final courses for my degree, which I am taking by distance education; statistics and nursing administration and sociology. I push myself to accomplish these things, to stay up and to cope. I must be there for my daughter and my husband and the rest of my family. I must.

Nicola is at my elbow now, whining to be picked up. I stand and reach for her, nestling her into my arms. She beams at me with complete love and trust, her eyes a deep sapphire next to the blue shirt she is wearing.

"Will you hold me? Will you read to me?" Nicola asks.

Together we sit on the couch. I slouch, resting my head on the back cushions. She gives me a book called *Annie and the Wild Animals,* one of her favourites. It has bright Nordic floral designs and tiny detailed pictures bordering each page. Nicola is a comforting warmth on my lap in her pink fleece pyjamas.

Annie is lonely because her cat has disappeared. She decides to make corn cakes for the animals of the forest. One by one they come, getting brasher and brasher as the story goes on. When her cornmeal is all gone and they try to invade her house, Annie realizes that these wild animals are not capable of being pets.

Nicola cringes with delight at the picture of the giant moose pushing his head through Annie's window, and at the grizzly rearing up and roaring hungrily. She has other books showing bears as sailors, bears setting up a tea party, bears picnicking in the woods with children.

I don't like the roaring grizzly or these chummy bears that take on the mannerisms of people. When I get a handful of jelly bears, I always bite their heads off first. When we visit the zoo, I pretend to punch the statue of a grizzly in the nose, and everyone laughs. When we visit Trevor's mom and stepdad in Canmore, I turn their three-foot-high brown teddy upside down and backwards in the urn that holds their collection of stuffed animals.

Nicola wants the story again. I suggest *The Three Little Kittens*.

Trevor and I talked briefly before he fell asleep tonight. He thinks my dad has only a couple more years to live, and I am angry at this guess of his. I tell him about my sister Mary. He agrees to look at a list of her medications to see if they are out-of-line. He'll be away on Saturday, he tells me. He and Brian are going ice climbing. I don't mind, do I? I tell him it's fine, knowing I will spend most of the day in bed after setting Nicola up at the kitchen table with some felt pens and a packet of Jell-O powder in a bowl for her to lick off her fingers. I want to ask him if he loves me, but I dread the automatic "of course" he will offer.

I give up on sleep to prowl through the silence of our night-time house. I'm glad Trevor will be away this weekend. It's more and more of a strain to act as if I am doing fine when he's around. This way I can let go, let the deep sadness just be there. I will stay away from my mother and my sisters, who will know how low I am and want to talk about it. I don't really know what's wrong. A part of it is the constant hurting, the unrelenting physical pain.

Earlier today Nicola and I visited the library. A little boy in the children's section kept glancing up from his book and looking at me, squinting his eyes or covering first one eye and then the other. When Nicola left my lap to wander on her own, he came and sat beside me. "What happened to your eye?" he asked.

Beside us on the wall was a poster of a large pale-blond grizzly walking at the edge of a rain forest. I gestured to it and answered matter-of-factly, "I was bitten by a bear."

Before he could respond, a woman grabbed at his arm, pulling him from the tiny child's chair. "Don't talk to people you don't know," she admonished him. Then she shot a venomous look at me. "Why would you scare a child with a story like that?"

Wrapped in a blanket, I climb into the padded window-seat in our dining room. I think about the home Trevor and I will build someday. We play with the idea of making it look like an old train station, with a porch, gabled dormers and multipaned windows. We'll move somewhere smaller, probably to a little mountain town in British Columbia. It is something Trevor and I share, this hope for a new life on the clean slate of a new town.

I go back to bed, crawling in beside Trevor's warm body. I trace his face with my finger, ever so lightly. He's had surgery to straighten his nose, and its silhouette as he breathes heavily into the dark is a big improvement on the crooked, sunken fighter's nose I used to see. It's made of a bone graft, right to the end; Dr. Lewis borrowed some of the ulna from Trevor's forearm. The bone pokes when we try to kiss each other. Suddenly, I wish with vehemence that I looked like I used to. I would love for Trevor to wake to the surprise of my balanced and pretty face.

I've had a pregnancy test, and it is positive. No one wants to believe me when I say it is twins. But I know. I felt ovulation pains on both sides.

The ultrasound technician is skeptical. She moves the scanner casually over my stomach.

"Yeah. There's the fetus. It looks fine. So many patients come through here hoping to find they're carrying twins. But they're just big for their due dates."

"Please," I say nervously. "Have another look."

She places the scanner and looks again. Her brow furrows. "Hey, there are two. You do have twins." She wipes her hands without looking at me, then scans some more. Makes notes. "You can get changed now. Out the door and to your right."

I lie unmoving, momentarily stunned. Twins. It is true. Oh my God. Once I'm dressed, I head for the payphones to call Trevor at the medical clinic.

"Trevor? It really is twins. We're having two babies. Two!" I am crying. "How are we going to do it?"

He is ecstatic. He laughs outright, and I can hear him pounding on the table in front of him. "We'll do fine. We can both feed, and I'll do diapers. How wonderful! A baby for each arm!"

On the way home, I pick up two white roses.

By thirty-eight weeks, I am so enormous I have difficulty walking. Driving to pick Nicola up at her playschool, I have to slide the front seat back to make room for my huge dinosaur egg of an abdomen. I cover the last half a block on foot, aware of how preposterous I look. I struggle to hold my dress out from my body, but it flies back at me, plastered against my shape by the strong wind to display my front in all its glory.

Two cars are driving along beside me. The one in front stops. But the driver in the car behind is gawking at me, mouth agape. I gesture to warn him, but there isn't time, and with his head still swung in amazement in my direction, he drives right into the car ahead of him.

I am afraid for the baby on the right, which hardly moves. The doctor tells me not to worry; some fetuses don't move very much. Almost, I allow myself to be reassured. But the feeling stays. Something is wrong.

In labour, I am impatient. Get my babies out. Let me see them. I laugh with the nurse, breathe, push, obey. Inside, I'm tight with anxiety.

Daniel arrives wailing, red and tight, waving angry limbs. The second baby is turned sideways and is in distress. The doctor makes a quick decision to turn the baby around by putting her hands inside me. I moan with the pain. I want to slide right through the wall behind me to escape the tremendous pressure between my legs.

The second twin is hauled out with forceps. She's grey, flaccid, soundless.

Doctors and nurses cluster around our new baby girl. The room is hushed. Instruments click. People's faces are serious.

I peer from my flat-on-the-back position, around Trevor's body at my side. "What's wrong? What's going on?"

Trevor lowers his face to kiss my brow. "Well done, my love. You did it. We've got two!"

I'm holding one sleeping, wrinkled, little-old-man-faced bundle in my arms. I smile at him, then crane desperately for a look at the isolette beside us. Through a gap between the bodies I see my second baby lying on the special table, limbs splayed, head extended back. For a moment I can see her little face. "Oh, no!" My cry is weak. "She's got Down syndrome. Look. Oh, Trevor, Down syndrome."

"No, she's fine, love." He bends to kiss me again. "She's just funny-looking because she's had a hard time."

I shake my head. Now I know what was wrong.

The minutes pass as the staff tidy me up and work on our little girl. Finally our family doctor advances cautiously, pulling off her gloves. "I'm afraid it looks as though your little daughter has Down syndrome." She is gentle and quiet, her eyes full of compassion.

Trevor and I stare at each other in shock. The baby needs oxygen, IV, the warmth of the isolette. Trevor's tears fall on my unmoving face.

The hospital days are full: geneticist, pediatrician, general practitioner, obstetrician, cardiologist, social worker, liaison nurses, postpartum nurses, nursery staff, family, friends. On the second day, orthopedics is needed as well. Ellen also has clubbed feet, both of them twisted up onto her shin bones. They will operate, cast her and give her special shoes with a brace later, when she is moving.

Two babies to feed and care for.

I tire very quickly of people's attempts to console me. "They're such special children." "She'll be such a blessing." "They are so good-natured." "You were chosen by God. He never gives you more than you can handle."

In the daytime I carry on. I cry with Trevor, when we're alone, but there's always someone coming in, reassuring. I don't want to be reassured. I want to be angry. I learn to live minute by minute until I can let my feelings go in the long, dark nights. I turn down the nurse's offer of a back rub, knowing her touch might make me cry. I can't stand the thought of more empty reassurance.

Why has this happened? Why? I want to trust the world, but I can't. I need to be on guard constantly for the next bad thing.

I have nightmares of dead babies and of twisted, deformed faces and limbs.

Maybe she'll just die.

But I want two. I want my matched set. I want my pretty pictures of two happy babies learning to crawl, to walk, to talk together. Two kids at school, riding bikes, going to dances. Twins. I want the specialness. But I don't want a child who will look different. Trevor and I already look different. More stares.

Daniel nurses well and often. He's a grumpy little fellow with a sour, red face. He curls into me, clutches firmly at my finger and gazes deep blue eyes at the world.

Ellen needs oxygen. She has difficulty sucking, with her protruding tongue and flaccid little mouth. Her head lolls heavily from side to side. But she's so pretty when she's all pinked up. Her eyes slant in a clear, blue tilt. Her hair is red-gold. She's a peaches-and-cream little one. With Down syndrome.

I rage. I don't want more boulders to climb over. I don't want more grief to cope with. How will I ever handle this, with my blues, my illnesses and pain, my father's cancer? Is it fate? A God in the heavens pulling strings on earth?

At night I cry and cry until I am empty. Finally, I sleep.

Sarah has knit delightful little vests and bomber-style hats for our two seven-pounders. Trevor and I sit on the hospital bed, holding a dressed-up baby each. Click. A nurse takes our smiling picture.

Once we're home from the hospital, there are many appointments to attend. Physiotherapists. Speech therapists. Audiologists to make sure Ellen can hear. Orthopedists for her twisted feet. The corridors of Children's Hospital are wide and bright with banners and pictures. There is a wall-to-wall fish tank that entrances Nicola. Trevor and I sit, beaten and exhausted, waiting for the pediatrician. It is more work than we could have imagined to manage three children. Our grief about Ellen wastes us. We have such anger but won't admit to it.

Dr. Fagan is dark-haired, with glasses and a genial, welcoming smile. He instructed Trevor in pediatrics at medical school.

"Trevor and Patricia. Please come through. And these are your children. They're beautiful."

I am taken aback. Dr. Fagan is not what I expected. He looks at each of us when he speaks. He shakes both our hands.

His holding and unwrapping of Ellen is infinitely gentle. He smiles down at her, speaking softly and crooning, looking deep into her fascinated eyes. He handles her as though she were precious and wondrous. We watch. We soak it up. We are given a lesson in valuing her.

Ellen is healthy and well, he tells us. There aren't any of the heart defects common in children with Down syndrome. She will be developmentally slow, and will learn to walk, talk and feed herself later than other children. She will be able to go to school, and with special assistance will learn to read and write. She could grow up to be independent, have a job, possibly even a relationship. I am stunned. I had pictured an institution like the one where my sister Mary has lived since her teen years.

The babies sleep together in the big cradle Trevor built, Daniel squalling as Ellen, eyes wide, sucks contentedly on his earlobe. I change Ellen's diapers gently and slowly now. I hum songs and speak to her. I hold her heavy head with care when I feed her.

Trevor and I sit on the couch, Ellen and Daniel held between us. We look into their little faces, caress the downy fuzz that is their hair. They grasp our fingers with promise. Individuals, not twins. Let Ellen have odd facial features and be slow developmentally. It's who she is. I will try to let her be. Let them be. And love them both.

My father is dying.

His hospital room is identical to the ones Trevor and I were in after our accident. It is the same as the rooms I've worked in as a nurse. Yellow bedspread. Yellow-and-orange plaid curtains. The winter light shines dimly through the panes.

Mom sits on a chair at the bedside, brittle. I lean over my father and tidy the covers, straighten his pillow. His lips, cracked and dry, curve upward in pleasure.

"The doctor has told me what I might die of." His voice is weak and small. "My platelets and hemoglobin are very low. It might be a hemorrhage, or a heart attack, or an infection. We just have to wait and see."

"Oh, Dad."

"I might be able to come home. They're talking about it. I could die in my own bed."

Mom doesn't have much to say later, when we discuss it. But what matters most to everyone is that Dad die feeling accepted, loved, supported. No more beepers and intercoms and needles and staff that changes every shift. Within days, he is nestled in his bed at home, with the old flannelette sheets and wool blankets he's used to, in the back bedroom he and Mom have shared for so long.

I am exhausted. Close to tears at every move. I'm restless and on edge with Trevor. So much of my anger is directed his way. His gestures, suggestions and comments irritate me. Mom is tightlipped and withdrawn, and sometimes Dad snaps at her.

He deteriorates quickly. He's short of breath, confused, groggy. He can't turn or eat or drink. Sometimes he's in terrible pain. He has a plaintive, childlike voice, craves comfort, is moaning and unmoving or restless and soaked in sweat.

I am fighting an infection in my face. I mop at my only eye. I am booked for another surgery. They will place a tiny glass tube into the tear duct. How will I be able to stand someone hurting my face again?

Painfully, I limp through the days, more and more short-tempered with Trevor, my one-year-old twins and my five-year-old daughter but always patient with my father and mother. Groceries and meals, laundry and cleaning.

My brothers and sisters come and fill the house. We are all waiting. I cry for my father, for my family, for myself. Dad's become weaker and more confused. He lies jaundiced and still, his eyes closed, his mouth open. In the slanting evening light I put my arms around him, resting my head on his chest. The room is silent when I leave, closing the door behind me.

I'm in a hospital room in Edmonton, three and a half hours north of Calgary, waiting for surgery on my eye. This is a new hospital to me. I am far from family and friends; lonely. Dressed in the thin blue cotton gown the nurse brought, I push the buttons to move my electric bed into a sitting position. My father's death is still raging within me. I cannot shake the finality of his being gone, and I refuse to accept it. Any moment now he will come into the room to visit me, hold my hand in his big, meaty one, offer to distract me with stories.

The little drainage tube they will place in my eye is made of Pyrex. It requires the tiniest of incisions, but the utmost care and precision in its placement. I am optimistic. If this tube works, I won't have to wipe at that eye as I have for the past seven years.

My roommate, brows high and inquisitive, nose pointing in my direction, asks for details when she finds out I've been mauled by a bear. I answer in short, clipped sentences, sure she will stop if I am rude. But she doesn't.

"They killed the bear? Oh, what a shame. Why didn't you

run away? My goodness, you climbed a tree, and still it got you. Did it claw you? Did it bite you? Did you have nightmares? Once when I was out camping with my family, we saw a black bear and he was . . ."

"I don't want to talk about it," I whisper finally.

"Oh." She sounds surprised. "Sorry. It was a long time ago, wasn't it? I didn't think it would bother you anymore."

Waking is not difficult. The anaesthetic was short, and I do not feel sick to my stomach. The pain is minimal. I am anxious to be on my way, to get out of this building full of illness and anonymous people.

The resident comes in for discharge instructions. He has a strong accent, and I can't understand most of what he says. Nor does he understand me. I shake my head in exasperation. I ask if we could have the nurse in to help us communicate, but he doesn't know what I am asking and chatters on. He is gesturing to the ointment that I place in my bad eye for lubrication and the stack of gauze patches the hospital has provided. I reach for the ointment.

"No, no, no!" He is forceful, taking the tube from my hand. His hands are cold. Holding firmly to the back of my head, he fills my damaged left eye with ointment and places a thick white patch on top. He tears off several long pieces of tape and criss-crosses them aggressively across the patch, from cheek to forehead.

"That's too much tape," I tell him. "Let me do it." He doesn't understand, and I decide to redo myself it as soon as he leaves. I reach to gather my ointment and patches together.

"No, no, no." He scowls at me, raising his finger in admonishment. Ointment in hand, he holds the back of my head again and proceeds to fill my good eye with the cream. "Hey!" I protest, blinded by the muck. But he is not done. I hear him fumbling with the package of patches, then feel a patch placed over my good eye. I sit, numb, as he rips off more tape and places it generously over the right side of my face.

I wait until he's done, then reach to pull at the tape. Instantly his hands are on mine, stopping me.

"How am I supposed to get home? I can't see!"

He pats me on the shoulder, and then he's gone. I hear the nurse come in.

"Look what the resident did." I start to laugh.

"Well, he must want it that way for a reason."

"Do you rent out Seeing Eye dogs, then?"

I peel off the patches so I can clean up the muck of ointment and see where I am going. Home.

The children are in bed, and Trevor and I sit together in the living room. We each have a sketchpad and we work in silence, drawing plans for our new house. I can't plan with him, as his strong ideas overpower mine. We will move in a couple of years, when my health problems have straightened out and Trevor has worked enough extra shifts at his medical clinic for us to afford it.

"Trish. Are you ready? I want to show you."

I slide over beside him. He has drawn out a small two-bedroom apartment that will be built into the roof of the garage. "See, I've given you dormers and sloped ceilings. We'll do wainscotting, too, like in your magazine pictures. I can take some time off and build this first. Then we can live in it while I build the big house beside it."

I study his drawing. "It looks wonderful. But how long would we have to live there? It's not a very big space."

"Oh, not long. Once I get building, you'll see."

"I've drawn a kind of a sunroom."

"A sunroom? For the big house? Where would it go?"

"I think off the living room."

"We can do it. Dream on. I love seeing the light in your face every time we plan the house or you go looking at fabrics."

I settle back on the couch, pulling my sketches to my chest. "I feel so guilty. I should be happier as a wife. And I should feel more satisfied as a mother. I wanted children, and we have three gorgeous ones. I need to accept Ellen more."

Trevor sits up straight, twisting his pencil in his hands. "You are so hard on yourself, Trish."

"Why do I need to shut down for most of each day? I'm not adventuresome. I have no endurance. I'm not who you married. I'm not pretty anymore. How can you still love me?"

"Well . . . ," he says, "you're still tall." We are incredulous for a moment, then laugh together.

"Hey, come here." He gestures. I lean sideways onto his shoulder. He's wearing his holey, scratchy gardening sweater. "Remember, I'm different too. We're both crooked." He traces a circle on the palm of my hand. "Mom told us years ago we're not facially disfigured. We're facially distinguished."

"Mmmhmm." I sigh. For a long time we just sit.

"I want to go climbing this Saturday," he says finally. "You could come up to Canmore and stay with Mom and Jac. They'd be glad to see you. I'd be around in the evening, and Mom could help you with the kids."

I think it over. "Maybe I could take the double stroller, and the kids and I could go walking on the dike beside the river. If I bring the dog with me, I won't be so nervous about bears."

"Aw, Trish, so many people walk by the river. You won't have to worry about bears."

"I know that rationally, but it's just being in the mountains, with the evergreen trees and that certain smell in the air. It triggers fear. I wish we could hike in New Zealand again. No animals to watch for."

"Let's go to bed." He stands in front of me, reaching forward with both hands to pull me to my feet. "And don't go sneaking off to the basement tonight if you can't sleep or want to cry. I will hold you. Let me."

"We'll have hollyhocks growing right outside the kitchen windows, and the windows will be tall wood ones that swing outward. Wouldn't that be perfect?"

"You're changing the subject on me." He pulls me to him. His hand strokes my hair. "We'll have delphiniums too," he says, "beautiful big blue ones."

I stand at our patio doors and look out. Trevor has won an award from the Horticultural Society for the work he has done in our yard. He's built a curving deck with stone staircases and retaining walls, and a sunken brick terrace with an arched gate into it. Shrubs and new trees fill the corners. Flowers bloom everywhere. It is truly beautiful. I crane my neck to peer to the upper yard where the children's sandbox and swing are. Nicola has made a tent of an old bedspread for the twins, and they are sitting on the grass eating animal crackers. I have just brought them home from my mother's. I turn, assured they are all right, and return to the pillows I have piled at one end of the couch.

The tears won't stop today. The ache in my face and head has been worsening. Four times now the surgeon has gone into the sinuses on the left side of my face and tried to clean up the infection. But it only works for a month or two, then the sinuses infect again. I seem to be continually on antibiotics. I am worried about my stagnant left eye, too. It has been hurting, and now there is drainage as well. I wonder how long it will last. Can it sit there forever, unmoving and protected by ointment and a graft of muscle and skin?

The front door squeaks as Trevor comes in. "Hello, my sore wife." He crosses the living room in a couple of steps and leans to kiss my forehead. "Where are the kids?"

"In the yard."

"You've been crying?"

"I can't seem to do anything but be sick these days."

"You've created three children. Gorgeous children. Right?" I can tell he is trying to humour me. I don't think he wants to hear about my day. My pain. My crying.

"There's no supper. Sorry."

"Are you getting infected again?"

"Yes. Chills, aching, and I'm dead tired. I'm worried about my eye, too. It's so sore." I push my face into the pillows. "I'm sorry."

"Stop being sorry. Take it easy tonight. You can go to bed early."

"No. I've got a meeting. AboutFace."

My photograph stares up from a newspaper article in front of me: "Scars Run Deep Years after Attack: Local Woman Forms Support Group." I've started a Calgary chapter of AboutFace, a national organization for people with facial differences that provides information, support and training opportunities. For the past year I've met monthly with members to share stories and build hope for more respectful treatment in our appearance-conscious society. I want to be at tonight's meeting because some new people will be there. Sometimes parents of children with a facial disfigurement are taken aback when they meet facially disfigured adults. They want to believe that their child's scarring or facial anomaly is curable, and the adult members of AboutFace are living examples of the limits and potential of plastic surgery. Our group has a school information program planned, and I will go out to talk to some hospitals. On a good day. On a better day. Today I just have to show up.

Trevor goes to the window to check on the children, then comes back to sit next to me. "You're ill, Trish. I think you should stay home."

"I have to go. I'm supposed to be the leader!"

Trevor moves into the kitchen. I hear pots banging. "Go lie down. Get some sleep," he yells. He doesn't know that I have been in bed all day.

"Are you angry?"

"I think you're crazy. Go lie down. You only have an hour or so."

Holding my head very still and straight, I walk slowly down the newly carpeted hall, past the inevitable baskets of laundry. In the silence of our bed, I wrap myself in the double wedding ring quilt my parents gave us. I will take my antibiotics and painkillers and I will get through the evening. I have to prove to myself I am good for something.

Dr. Cook, my new ear, nose and throat doctor, thinks he can help me. New techniques and equipment let him see inside the sinuses as he works, he says, with a tiny fibre-optic scope. He has miniature tools that allow him to get at infection and scar tissue. I find myself smiling at this fast-talking doctor who moves about with unbridled energy, accepting his explanations about why another surgery might help. Hope washes over me.

A month later, the surgery is a fait accompli. Number fifteen since the accident, I think. I've lost track. After several hours I am discharged home, still comfortably full of the cocaine they spray for local anaesthesia. My discharge teaching sheet is blank except for a huge scrawl across the middle of the paper: "Remove packing in A.M."

When I awake the next day, the painkillers have worn off and the pain is intense. I sit, supported by a pile of pillows, upright on our spindle bed. The children stand in a line beside me, staring at the gauze protruding from my nostrils.

Nicola, now six, takes my hand in hers. "Do you feel better?"

I groan, smiling at the same time. I very cautiously move my head to the side to look at her open face and inquisitive blue eyes. Ellen pushes a stuffed rabbit into my arms. "Here," she says in her garbled speech.

Trevor comes in, pulling Daniel up onto the bed and tickling him for a minute. "Hey. Stop that," I complain.

"Trish, I talked with Dr. Cook. He says the surgery should

make a huge difference. You were full of scar tissue, especially on the left side where the bear laid your face open. What he did was pretty extensive, so you'll be awfully sore for a couple of weeks, but this should make a big difference to your pain and congestion and infection in the long run."

All the children have climbed onto the bed. Ellen wants her rabbit back. But it is really Daniel's rabbit, and with a strong pull he yanks it from Ellen's grasp. She howls, throwing herself face down. Trevor takes the twins out. They are back in a moment, with a stuffed animal each.

Trevor sits down beside me, reaching for the packing.

"Wait," I say. "Should the kids be here? And maybe we should have a bucket in case it bleeds." I wish I could be absent for what is about to happen. "How much packing is there?"

Trevor leaves the room and comes back with an ice-cream bucket. "I think the kids will be okay."

Trevor pulls yards of blood-soaked gauze from my nose, dropping it into the bucket on my lap. The children gape. I yell. He stops when the bucket is half full. Blood pours from my nose as if from a faucet. His face is creased in concern, and the children's mouths form a line of little O's.

I take a deep shuddering breath, gauze hanging from my face. "Shouldn't an emergency department do this, or the doctor?" I ask angrily.

"I'll just keep going." Trevor's voice is quiet. He pulls, hand over hand. Blood flows, and I yell without thinking. When it is done, we look in silence at each other.

The twins have left for their bedrooms, where I can hear their voices in quiet play. Nicola comes around the bed, then climbs up to nestle into my shoulder. The room is still and dim, friendly and familiar. I settle into her softness.

My sister Mary has died. She choked during a seizure, and they could not get help to her fast enough. Would the help have been there on time if she had not been different-looking and mentally handicapped? Ambivalence stirs my insides. I took care of Mary when I was small. I helped her with the schoolwork she couldn't do. We lived in the same house, but she had her own world. How well did anyone know her? Who was she? What kind of a life was that to live? I want another chance. I want to love her better.

Auntie Gerry has had a stroke, and Trevor's friend Brent has died unexpectedly from complications with diabetes. I am flattened. Nothing seems to have meaning anymore. I spend my days waiting for time to pass, and there is nothing I want to do but be alone and sleep.

I am so afraid in the world. Afraid that the house will be broken into, afraid to walk in the park with my children, afraid to drive on busy roads. It feels constantly as if something else is going to happen to me or to us. I have nightmares of being attacked. Smiling faces drift towards me, then change so they are contorted, bloody, ravaged. They plague me, awake and asleep.

I'm on antidepressants and seeing a counsellor. I've tried stress therapy, sound and light therapy, the yeast diet, acupuncture, craniosacral therapy, reflexology and megavitamins. I've recorded my dreams, regressed to childhood, and listened to relaxation tapes. How can I curb these horrible dark feelings and fears? I just want to shut off. But I can't. Next week my left eye is to come out.

Through the door of my bedroom, even with a pillow folded over my ears, I can hear Trevor dressing the children in their outdoor clothes. He wants me to join them for an outing in our little row-boat. I don't want to go, but I know I should.

It is cold at the reservoir, in spite of the sun, and I am sorry to leave the warmth of the car. Bundled in fleece and hats, we make our way down to the rocky beach. The children are quarrelsome today. Daniel stumbles getting into the boat and begins to cry. Ellen decides she wants Trevor to hold her and lets out a loud wail. Nicola faces me, seated in the bow, her face unusually stormy. I fight my pain and fear and recite to myself that the boat won't tip. We'll be safe this time. We'll be safe. I push the image of my children floating face-down from my mind.

"Can you get those kids to stop crying?" Trevor snaps, wet to his ankles as he manoeuvres the small craft into deeper water.

"No." I scowl. "I can't."

The boat finally floats and Trevor hops in so he can row. Away we drift, across smooth waters. The twins have quietened, but they continue to cry. I close my eye, trying to imagine myself back in my bed. The left side of my head throbs unrelentingly.

From a slow drift, the boat lurches to a halt. Trevor plunges the oars in to get us moving again. Reluctantly, the little craft creeps forward, then stops. "A shallow spot," he says, glowering. He uses the oars as levers, pushing them into the weedy silt. He's using all his strength, but the boat moves only inches. He heaves himself over the side of the boat into shin-deep muddy water and wades around to the bow, where he grasps and pulls.

"I want to go home!" Nicola wails. The twins increase their cries. Trevor is hauling on the boat, his feet jamming in the muck.

Suddenly I am laughing. I can't help myself. Trevor, looking back, catches the ear-to-ear grin on my face. His glower dissolves, and he stands still in the icy water to throw his head back, laughing with me. I move one arm to blow him a kiss. He leans into the rope again, exaggerating the suck and pull of the mud on his legs, and sings loudly over the children's cries, hauling us back to shore.

The hospital scene is so familiar, though this is a hospital I have never been to before. Dr. Copithorne looks more like an up-and-coming business executive than a doctor specializing in plastic surgery on eyes. He has explained to me that I will be left with a small dip in my face where my left eye used to be, and that I may be able to be fitted for a prosthesis later. His smile is disarming, and I tentatively allow myself to trust his words. Having none of its natural defences, my eye is rotting, and six months of antibiotics have not been enough to preserve it. Two different eye specialists have recommended this procedure, warning that I could risk abscesses, septicemia and even brain damage otherwise. Yet a part of me remains terrified. I don't know if I can take more pain or changes to my appearance. The doctor's visit is brief, so I seek comfort in my nurses. But they are efficient and jollying. I am brave, they tell me. Just look at all I have been through.

Later, I push the call bell. I ask the nurse to sit with me. She returns with some Ativan. I let the tiny pill melt under my tongue, waiting to be delivered into its soft escape.

It is over, they tell me. I see figures across the room. Little purple shapes dance around the rim of my vision. I call out, but I am alone in my room.

My eye. That sick, infected, messy ache in my head. Gone? My hand travels through time to reach my face. The empty socket is stuffed with gauze taped to the side of my face. Never have I felt such pain. How can that be? A bear chewed on my head, destroyed bones, skin, muscle and half my scalp, and never have I felt such pain. I whimper in desperation, finally finding the call button in my drugged haze.

The nurse is abrupt. "Here now! I'm coming as fast as I can. What's that you're saying? No, you can't have anything more for pain. You've an hour to go yet."

I shut the doors to my heart and pull deep, deep within to that place of simply existing. I turn away from myself and my agony.

Rounds. The doctor comes to see how his patient is doing. The first day he comes right to my bedside. Sees me stiff on the bed, bloody gauze covering the new hole in my head, my mouth twisted and crying. I make the mistake of looking directly at him with my right eye, beseeching him for relief, caring. Every day after that he comes only to the door, asking brightly from there how things are going.

I have had so much pain already. Shouldn't I be good at this? My visitors are awkward and distant, and they leave as soon as they can. No one wants to be witness to this suffering.

Trevor and I travel together at the end of the week to the hospital complex on the hill. It will be my old friend, our original plastic surgeon, who will remove the packing from my eye socket and check that all is well in the orbit.

The doctor is gentle as he peels away the layers of tape. He works in quiet concentration. Trevor holds a basin into which the packing is dropped piece by piece. The doctor dips some clean gauze in sterile water and soaks off the final stubborn clots. I smile, but he doesn't smile back. As he finishes, he and Trevor glance quickly at each other, then at me. The doctor looks down and away, gesturing to the door.

"The washroom's through there."

Patch in hand, I turn to go, smiling at Trevor to lighten the atmosphere. He smiles too, but his look is guarded. I hear the two men's voices in quiet conversation as I step into the bathroom and close the door.

"Uggh." It is involuntary, as though I have been kicked in the stomach. I reach to lean on the counter. "Oh, my God. Oh, God, what have I done?" I stare at the bruised and bloody hole in the side of my face, blinking as fast as I can to still the threatening tears. It is as though I am looking at a skull. It is me. My pulse is pounding loudly, and there's a rushing in my head. I shake myself, unable to stop looking in the mirror. The hole is shadowed and bruised, and so much deeper than I had expected.

Removing the backing from a new patch, I place it over the opening. I am not sure it will be big enough to cover this deformity, but it is. I take an enormous breath and turn back to the examining room.

"I guess that's it," I say to the two expectant faces.

"It's healthy," the doctor says.

After awkward good-byes, Trevor and I file out in silence, hand in hand. We walk down the familiar hallway. At the elevator, Trevor pushes the button and turns to me. "Are you okay?"

I nod. "I'm fine." My voice cracks. I can't keep up the pretence. Tears come, and great wracking sobs. Trevor's arms close around me, his face pushed into my hair. "Trish. Oh my Trish. Oh love." We cling to each other, while the elevator comes and goes and the horror in my heart gives vent.

Eventually, I will be able to get a prosthesis made. If I had lost simply my eye and not my eyelids, I could have a glass eye, which would fit into the socket. But because my lids are gone I will need a total prosthesis: eyeball, lids and brow made from a rubbery, lifelike compound.

Through my AboutFace group, I hear of a woman named Rhianna who lost her eye and lids to cancer. She has a prosthesis like the one I am considering, so I arrange a meeting. The morning she arrives, I stand at the front door in the frigid air to greet her. Excitement curls around my insides. Symmetry and balance again for my face! Rhianna keeps her face low as she manoeuvres the slippery sidewalk. Is she shy? How is she feeling about being examined and interrogated? At the bottom of the stairs she looks up to say hello.

"Close the door! We're not heating the whole outside, you know," yells Trevor playfully from the kitchen, just as I feel my breath catch in my throat at seeing Rhianna's face. As I usher her in and take her coat and hat, we talk politely, nonsensically, with each other. I want to gawk. Her prosthesis looks very real, but the skin around it doesn't match that of her cheek, pink in the winter chill, and it does not move. Her good eye softens as she smiles in my direction, while the prosthesis stares stiffly ahead. I couldn't. I couldn't possibly. I am flooded with disappointment.

Rhianna is quiet-spoken, and she works to put me at ease. With tea and cookies in front of us and Trevor minding the children at the other end of the house, we speak candidly. She describes the year and more of surgeries, and the building and fitting of the prosthesis. She removes her prosthesis, showing me the bolts sticking out of her brow and cheekbones. Magnets on the back of the prosthesis hold it to her face. I sneak glances at the hollow where her eye used to be.

Standing in front of the bathroom sink, I hold Rhianna's prosthesis to my face. But it is the wrong eye, and we laugh with our reflections. She and I smile at each other in the small mirror, sharing our marred faces. I see only the balance in her face by now, the warmth and the life.

I am afraid to lie flat and be anaesthetized again, to have someone hurt my face by drilling bolts deep into my bones and deepening my orbit. I am afraid to hope. Yet I am tempted by optimism: this time it will work out, not hurt, not get infected. I see myself with a balanced face, shining on the world from two eyes once again. I will feel more normal, part of the world. I won't be as noticeable in public, and people will treat me with respect. Maybe I will look prettier. Oh, could I?

I have to go to another city for the prosthesis surgeries, hundreds of miles away from family and friends. At the hospital, I point out a tender area under my left cheekbone, a palpable lump, there since the sinus and eye infections. Should we investigate that first? I ask. Make sure there is nothing that might complicate things? I allow myself to be reassured. The low-grade fever, the ongoing pain, the incredible fatigue I feel are just remnants of the infections, just the result of emotional overload and parenting three small needy children.

My new surgeon doesn't come around before the operation. Instead, there is a young resident I have never seen before. To him, it's just another surgery. In my skimpy gown, I feel exposed and ugly as sin.

The resident is very good at not looking me in the eye. He gives yes and no answers in a monotone. I persist nonetheless. "You're going to be placing screws deep in the bone. There will be a tissue expander in my cheek to stretch out the undamaged skin so you can use it later to replace the scarred graft around my eye. You'll enlarge the orbit, too. I'm frightened of the pain. Could we plot this out beforehand and put some kind of pain-management plan in place?"

He chuckles, my youthful resident. I am an old woman to

him. "You are only having the orbit made a bit larger," he says. "There aren't many nerve cells there."

"What about the bone screws?"

"They don't *hurt*. The bones don't really feel. The insertion of the tissue expander is a simple, small procedure. It's usually done as a daycare procedure. Easy."

I stare at him, speechless for a moment. "Have you ever broken a bone? Have you ever had surgery?" I ask him.

"No."

You don't know what you're talking about. I think it, not brave enough to speak it aloud.

It hurts like hell, and the pain brings these past ten years flooding back. Hospital colours and smells and sounds. The metal kidney basin to vomit in. The blue cotton curtain pulled halfway around me. The click of the nurse's heels as she comes and goes. I hold my head very, very straight and still to lessen the discomfort. It's schizophrenic. The outside person and the hospital person. What have I ended up with? A gaping hole where my eye used to be. A tissue expander ready to be injected weekly with saline until it distorts my cheek. And three titanium bolts deep in my brow bone.

Back home in Calgary, I want to retreat like a squirrel in wintertime, take some food and drink and hide out under the blankets. But I make myself get out. My sister Margaret and I go to tiny restaurants and share our woes. When I berate myself, she reminds me of Popeye's slogan: "I y'am what I y'am and I likes what I y'am." We make jokes about our children, our husbands, our lives. Laughter lessens the pain and the fear. I visit my favourite store. The furniture and household accessories are a fantasy world for me to get lost in. In the fabrics department, I pull down the mammoth bolts of texture and colour and pattern. I wander the aisles and dream of the future, when Trevor and I and the kids will live in a new town in a new house with a wraparound porch and I will be coping just fine, with a matching set of warm and caring blue eyes.

I see a counsellor every week, and he is concerned about my fatigue and lassitude. Should I really be putting myself through this, he wonders? He gives me visualizations to relax into and asks me to keep a record of the horrific nightmares I fight.

In one of these, I am staying at a little cabin. It is sunny and lovely, and I am happy. The landscape is watercolours, white and blue and yellow. An old family car is there, and I climb in with Daniel. A large brown bear gets into the driver's seat and drives us away. I am relaxed. A country drive. But the bear takes us to a hospital. There are people talking to themselves, walking in circles, hunched over staring at their hands. Daniel is frightened and begins to cry. I try to tell him: Don't let them see that you are upset. Pretend you are all right. Don't swallow the pills they are giving you. Fight the restraints and the surgery. But Daniel is taken away from me, crying. I stare at the bear, pretending to be calm. He is the surgeon. He doesn't look at me, but the staff run at his beck and call. There are people walking around with their faces rearranged, their arms sewn to their heads, crying and wailing. The bear places me on the operating table, and I see the needle and the mask they will put over my face. His face is expressionless. Mine is too. I am terrified, but I must not satisfy him by letting him see how frightened I am. I must get away. The needle goes in, and then I am somersaulting backward into oblivion. There is a long endless scream, and it is me.

My cheek is swollen and disfigured. I visit my surgeon up on the hill, in the medical complex where my face began its metamorphosis so many years ago. He had advised against the prosthesis, and his manner is cool. He injects a small amount of saline each week. The headaches afterward have me throwing up, but I don't dare tell him. I want him to respect me again, to like me. In spite of my best intentions, the redness worsens, and the suture line begins to open and drain.

Trevor's taxed to the limit doing extra medical training. The kids are acting out. The house is a mess. I turn inward and stop my outings. When I am forced to leave the house for some reason, strangers stare and question me. "What happened? That looks so sore!" I swallow my four-times-daily doses of antibiotics and painkillers.

Overnight, my cheek blows out to a cherry-red, glistening and pustule-covered glob, well stretched of its own accord. The infection is called cellulitis. It has invaded the individual cells and could spread to my bloodstream. "The expander has to come out," my doctor says. "Immediately." Two more weeks in hospital on intravenous antibiotics. The children are shunted here, there and everywhere. But at least they get a chance to live with someone who gets up in the morning and doesn't try to break up fights from a bedroom hideout.

Immediately after the infection is cleared, it's time for another surgery. Back to the out-of-town hospital. We had planned initially to revise the scar across my forehead, raising the brow on the left side of my face and narrowing the thickened, scarred bridge of my nose. These procedures are omitted to simplify the process. Instead, the skin stretched out by the expander is pulled up to the orbit, and the skin graft that ran halfway down my cheek is gone. The three exterior bolts protrude through the skin, capped and ready for the magnets on the prosthesis. The orbit is discoloured and scabbed. I feel sick to my stomach gazing into that hole in my head. It is almost a year since I began this process. But it will be worth it in the end, I tell myself. I will be a new me.

It is time to create the prosthesis. The unit is furnished in soft colours and comfortable padded chairs. The staff are professional but caring, asking me about my family and how I am doing. I tell them about the constant pain, about my fear of hoping for too much, about being treated for depression. They jolly me along, assuring me that everything is going great. By the end of the first long day, I begin to relax.

Many long sessions later, I catch glimpses of the eye in process and see its blueness, pinkish skin tone and dark lashes. I have trouble sitting still in the surgeon's chair. My left cheek throbs, and my good eye wants to shut in fatigue. But hope keeps me buoyant, and the light, easy conversation of the staff bolsters my determination to be a positive part of the team.

The day comes. The prosthesis is completed. I am suddenly apprehensive, never having seen the full item. I would like some time alone to try it on, but this is not to be. The whole staff is called in. Even the receptionist is there. Everyone crowds around in front of the large mirror, smiling and nodding and talking all at once. The doctor snaps the prosthesis into place, then stands back. Everyone claps and congratulates me, leaning forward for a good look.

It is a horror movie. My mouth is smiling, but my hand wants to snatch this thing from my face and fling it far away in utter despair. The eye is small and partially turned inward. The lid is half shut, looking tired and worn-out; the lashes are cropped. The skin colour is tan. My cheek skin burns pink and hot.

All I can think of is getting out of here. I retreat deep inside, say my polite thank-you's and remove the eye to place it in the beige plastic carrying box they have given me. I will do what I always do. Hide.

In my motel room, I dive for the bed and weep and weep and weep, as I have not allowed myself to do in so long. I hold the little eye in my hand, close to my heart. My mind tries to block the turmoil of memories, to shake free of the waste of it all. Eventually, the crying stops. Disappointment encases me like concrete.

My face pain has escalated, though, and it wraps around my head. It almost stuns me with its severity. I think it must be the result of intense emotion, and hope with rest it will pass. Then suddenly, violently, I am sick to my stomach. I stagger to the bathroom. The room reels, and my vision is blurry. Stumbling back to bed, I pass a half wall of mirror and stop in shock. The entire left side of my face and down my neck is swollen a deep burgundy-red and covered with yellow pustules.

In the emergency department, there is rush and bustle. I am talking about my sister's dollhouse and my father's car as I fall slowly sideways off the examining table. Arms catch and support me, and the voices grow loud and hurried.

It is days before I am aware again. Cellulitis, they tell me. Septicemia. It spread into my bloodstream. They are very sorry, but they will have to remove the external bolts, the ones the prosthesis attaches to. They tell me they cannot replace those screws; there is too much risk of further infection. I have the prosthesis now, but I can never wear it, even if I want to. They will leave the inner bolts deep in the brow bone. These are inert, they say.

After ten days of intravenous antibiotics, I can go home to Calgary. Trevor and I have made our plans. In another three weeks, we will move to British Columbia. I will patch the deep hole in my face, and that is how the new community will know me. We will build our house and fill it with the beautiful colours and textures I have collected, and with our lives and our love.

V

The Dark Planet

From the foot of the narrow, dark-panelled staircase to my attic room, I hear their voices raised in argument.

"Daniel, you took her her drink the last time. It's my turn," Nicola cries.

"Let me go! I want to see Mommy too."

I pull the pillow over my head and curl in a fetal position. Trevor's voice cuts through the heavy air, imploring, "Shhh! Mom's trying to sleep. Nicola's turn. Go on. Take the drink up. And stay there until she drinks some." His voices softens. "And tell her I'll be up once you're in bed."

Nicola is eight. She moves lightly on the wooden stairs, on tiptoe, trying to avoid the creaks. She comes into the darkened room and crouches beside my bed. The blankets are strewn every which way. Mugs of soup and cups of juice sit untouched on the night table.

"Mommy?"

I remove the pillow from my head. I feel hollow.

"Mommy? Are you okay?"

I reach for her hand, my face turned into the mattress.

"I drew a picture for you. It's you and me. We're on a date. Holding hands. You have a basket of flowers." She grips my hand tightly. "I brought you a drink."

I turn my head, open my eyes, and look dully at her expectant face. I move my mouth into a small smile, feeling as though I am looking at her from the wrong end of a telescope. Darkness blankets me as her little feet go cautiously down the attic stairwell.

❧

The house we are renting in Napier, British Columbia, is small and shadowy inside from the towering cedar trees that surround it. We've been staying here for the past eight months, while Trevor builds a garage on our land, taking time off from being a doctor. On top of the garage will be the two-bedroom suite he designed. We'll live there until the main house is ready.

The land we're building on is high on a hillside, with wonderful views of a long, thin lake stretching between mountain peaks.

Our house will be less than a block from the hospital where Trevor has a job lined up in the emergency department. We'll be able to walk along tree-lined streets, past beautiful old wooden houses, to the downtown: restaurants, the library, the theatre. Our land is surrounded by empty lots, and we will soon discover it is also home to skunks, deer, racoons and the occasional bear and cougar. Yet Napier feels welcoming and safer than the city. Its population is small, the pace is slow, and in the hundred years the town has existed, there have been no attacks by bears on humans, as far as I know. I can look realistically now at the statistics on bear encounters and accept that, as long as I take precautions, it is unlikely I will even see one.

But I have been heavy with grief since we arrived here, fighting to stay afloat in a sea of pain and sadness. For months, I pulled my body with me like a great, aching sack as I shopped for groceries and attended meetings at Nicola's school. Now I do not even have the energy for that. We've put the twins in daycare, and I've stopped answering the phone. Trevor and I yell a great deal, and there are times when our house is poisoned with our unhappiness. I've started to camp out in the dark attic space.

Our family doctor and Trevor talk, and they decide we are fooling ourselves to think that my problems are due simply to the pain and infections. Trish is very depressed, they say. But the antidepressants I'm prescribed have no effect.

I get up sometimes and move into the outside world, to sit on our big beige couch and hold a book on my lap for Ellen. I join my family for supper, just to be there, staring at my plate while the children fight over who gets to sit next to me.

Trevor fills in all that I don't do. He is super Dad, single-parenting, running the household, building our new home, and nursing me. He moves on automatic pilot, struggling to cope with the overload and trying not to explode. He offers me his arms when I join him in bed, and he wants me to talk to him, to say what I am feeling. But all I can speak of is hopelessness.

On the upstairs mattress, I think of suicide for the first time. My despair is unfathomable, terrifying, and it feels as if there is no way out, no one who can reach me. I have alienated my doctors by developing a chronic pain and infection pattern, with recurrent episodes of facial cellulitis. I mourn for the loss of their positive regard, their friendship, their powers.

I've been sick so long now, I don't know how to be well. I don't know what it is to feel good, to feel alive. I am shrinking and dying inside. I wait for the hours of the day to go by, and then the hours of the night. I rejoice only in the sleep the painkillers give me, a soft comforting blanket.

The footsteps on the stairwell are heavy, slow and measured. The floorboards creak, and the sound reminds me forcefully of my father's footsteps on the old floors of the house I grew up in. Trevor comes right to the mattress and signals me to move over.

"There's something I need to tell you," he says hesitantly.

"Some of my friends have advised me to stop being a martyr. They say I should leave you. But I can't. The reading I've been doing talks about acceptance. I need to love you just the way you are. I need to try."

Shame and guilt drown me from inside. I look at him dully.

"Would you go to a hospital? See a psychiatrist?"

I have to lick my lips over and over before they are moist enough for me to speak. "I'll go," I say. And then, "Don't tell anyone."

The psychiatric hospital, Hills Pavilion, is a one-hour drive from our home. Trevor, Ellen and Daniel are in the front seat, where Ellen has fallen asleep. She leans heavily over her father's legs. Daniel swivels right around to look at me in the back seat.

"Daddy, Mommy doesn't have her seatbelt on." No one answers him. He shoots a quick glance at his father's silent profile, then turns back to peer at me through the dark afternoon light. I lie with my face in my hands, my legs pulled up as far as I can get them.

"Mommy?" Daniel clutches the back of the front seat, like a bird clinging to a branch. Trevor takes one large hand from the steering wheel to reach for and cover Daniel's small one. Daniel's gaze is riveted on me. "Daddy, Mommy's crying."

"She's not feeling well. Sit straight so you're safe under your belt."

"But Mommy's not wearing hers. What if we have a crash?"

"We won't have a crash." Silence while Daniel rearranges himself facing the front. Trevor holds his hand again. "Your mom's been sick and sore so much that she's very sad. That's why we're taking her to a special hospital for a while."

For a moment there is only the sound of windshield wipers and wheels turning on the wet road. "Well," says Daniel with force, "if there was one thing I could wish for in the world, I wish you never got attacked by that bear."

The deadness that is my body starts to tremble. I am so sorry, so ashamed, so incredibly sad.

I am afraid of a new hospital and new staff. I have never been on a psychiatric ward before. Will the nurses at Hills Pavilion be warm and empathetic or judgemental? Will the doctor be an approachable person or a robot? Will I be forced to eat and drink? Will I be made to take drugs? I don't want anyone to know where I am going. We don't tell my mother.

Pink walls. Green chairs in a large room with shuffleboard and a pool table. Sliding doors to an outdoor patio and high-fenced lawn. The heavy doors of the unit are locked. The staff have the keys. Bedroom hallways stretch to the right and the left, men on one side, women on the other. There is a locked seclusion room at the end of each corridor.

I've had electroconvulsive therapy over the past two weeks. The doctors say it might pull me out of the pit I have disappeared into. Often there are four of us silently waiting our turns in the basement room painted swimming-pool green. In the room next door are curtained stalls with stretchers, machines with gauges, a psychiatrist, nurses, an anaesthetist. The procedure is the same each time. I lie on a thin, hard table. The staff laugh and talk as they attach electrodes to my temples. Afterward I am packaged up in a white blanket and wheeled back to the ward, mind thick and blurry.

ECT sometimes has what is called a "champagne effect." The first two treatments lift me out of depression to almost normalcy, but the effect fades, and in spite of more sessions, I hover somewhere just above catatonic. I spend hours staring at the fuzzy kittens in the pictures on the wall or watching the closed blinds vibrate in the air from the vent.

"Trish!" The voice is clipped, coming from behind me. I lie inert, face down in my pyjamas. "Trish!" The nurse comes into the room and pulls the covers from my back. I wish I could disappear.

"Get out of those pyjamas and into the tub right now. I've got it running. You're not going to your appointment with the doctor looking like that."

I sit up slowly, then stand. I pull away from the angry nurse when she reaches for my arm, surprised to see it is Fiona. She is usually so kind. I circle around her and head for the door at a run, crying and full of anger. She calls after me.

In the main seating area I find a chair and sit. I am dizzy and confused. I watch as Fiona sails right past me to the nursing station, ignoring me. Pauline, another nurse, dark-haired with seal-grey eyes, squats beside my chair.

"Trish." Her voice is quiet, and she strokes the back of my hand with her finger. "It's okay to stay in your PJs. Go back to bed if you like."

I sit, head in hands, trying to block out the people around me.

Rolled tightly into a protective ball on my bed, I stiffen at the sound of footsteps. "Trish? How are you doing?" It's Pauline. Her voice is soft and tentative.

I am cautious, my body and mind braced for an onslaught. I pull my soft spots deep within, curving my back and covering my face with my hands. Just like I did with the bear.

"Would you like a bath? I could give you a bubble bath and wash your hair for you." Her hand has found the curve of my shoulder. Its warmth is seductive. She remains there for a moment, her grasp holding solidly to my reluctance.

The washroom is cold metal, with a small tub in a partitioned stall. I stand fully clothed, shoulders hunched. My hair is on end, dirty and stiff.

Pauline pours creamy white liquid under the gushing hot-water tap. "Okay, in you go. Have a nice soak."

"I don't want you to see my body. I'm not usually this fat."

"I'm not even looking, love."

The caring in her voice as she coaxes me into the tub brings slow tears. She sings softly, rubbing a hot, wet cloth up my arms and over my shoulders. I fold my arms over my chest. I don't deserve this. I am bad.

"You are trying so hard. We all think so much of you," she says. "Do you know that?"

Her voice hums on. I sink into the warmth, letting the water and her touch caress me.

I am expected to participate in group outings and information sessions as well as daily occupational therapy. Some patients sit quietly, staring at nothing. Others are noisy and intrusive. I shake my head in dismay when I am offered a ceramic flowerpot to paint or plastic canvas to embroider with polyester wool.

Kate, the occupational therapist, asks if I would like to do a collage. She gives me a stack of magazines, and I cut and paste. An operating room. A bear. A baby. Hands. A woman screaming. A woman crying.

I feel prickles of happiness at plastering words and pictures onto a keepsake that will speak for me. I want to show it to everyone, have them notice the size and strength of the bear, the cold instruments in the operating-room photo, the exquisite tenderness of the hands holding the baby. But the others simply nod or look away after a quick glance.

"That's nice," Kate says, oblivious to the tension running through me. "Now, what would you like to do next?"

When no one is watching, I leave. I walk robotlike to my

bed, hands clutching at the torment that is in my head: bloody faces and dead babies and an endless wail filling what had been a dead space. I shake from head to toe, craving the peace of no feeling again.

Sometime later, a nurse comes into my room. She sits beside me on the bed, her hand moving softly up and down one of my arms. "I know a story about bears," she says. "An Indian legend. If you are attacked by a bear and survive, then you gain the wisdom, the power and the healing abilities of the bear that attacked you. There is a story of a young Native boy who was mauled terribly but lived, and they say he couldn't be injured again in any way. He was filled with the bear's power. Forever."

My ragged breaths slow. Somewhere down the hall, a door slams.

❦

I will be discharged home yet again from Hills Pavilion after my eighth admission in a year and a half. Before I leave I have an interview with the psychiatrist. He settles himself in his stiff upholstered chair and looks at me, puzzled.

"You didn't participate in the group sessions, Kate tells me. You sat in but wouldn't take part. What's up? You're supposed to be ready to go home."

"I feel so listless." I look at my feet in Birkenstock sandals. My dress billows large, covering my bulk. I've put on sixty pounds since starting the Lithium and Epival they've prescribed as mood stabilizers. "I don't want to be with anyone."

"How do you feel about going home, then?"

"I'm scared. I can't seem to be what I'm supposed to as a mother. I'm not present for Trevor as a wife. I get overwhelmed at home." There is silence. "I'm so tired of being sick. Why can't I just snap out of it?"

"You've been sick a long time, Trish, and it will take a long time to get well. You've had so many things to deal with: facial disfigurement, chronic pain, family deaths. You've moved to a new town, away from family and supports, and you and Trevor are living with three children in a very small space."

Trevor finished building the apartment six months ago. We've stored our belongings in the garage and moved into the six hundred square feet above. It is a lovely place, with wood wainscotting and sloped ceilings and built-in bookcases, but tiny for five of us.

"Still, lots of people have difficulties and don't fold like I do."

"Be patient with yourself," he says. "And Trish: you've got to stop using your medication to escape your feelings. It's dangerous." I don't answer. "You know," he continues, "you don't need more psychotherapy. What you need is an experience of hope."

He wishes me well, and I am dismissed. Until the next time.

Nicola, ten now, has constructed a mailbox of art paper and attached it to my bedroom door. When I am low and shut myself away from the children, they drop pictures and notes into the cardboard folder.

I lie in my room with the door locked, my face throbbing. My eye socket is inflamed and tender again. But Trevor is on call, and the homecare worker who helps with the children is set to go home at any moment. I must get up.

The children have built tents with their bedclothes in the small play space. Two baskets of laundry anchor the ends. Around the corner in the kitchen, they have taken over the counter and table with art projects. Crayons and felts, scissors and glue are everywhere.

Ellen, sucking her thumb, pushes against me, saying, "I want a hug." Daniel pushes too, struggling to get under my arm. Nicola stands off to one side. "Leave her alone, you guys," she says. "Are you okay, Mommy?"

I open my arms to them. "Would you like to go to the beach for supper? We could get hot dogs and sit on a blanket." It is the only way I can think of to escape the mess and the realities of home.

"Hooray!"

"Yes!"

"Could we go to Dairy Queen after?"

Pocketing my medications, I reach for their hands.

Since we moved here, I have had six medical hospital admissions for the infections in the left side of my face and neck. The internist in our small town has had me flown to the larger Calgary hospital twice for treatment and investigation. One specialist placed me on a two-month intravenous antibiotic program. Conscientiously I carried the bags, tubing and medications wherever I went, hooking the pole up at home as I held my little ones on my lap for stories, circling around it in the kitchen while I made lunches and set the table. One week after the treatment was complete, I was hospitalized again with cellulitis.

The infectious disease consultants have advised that all the screws, wires and implants in my face be removed. The surgeons don't believe more surgery would help, doggedly insisting the hardware is not the source of the problem. Over and over again, they suggest treatment with antibiotics. The lump behind my left-cheekbone rib graft does not appear on scans, and therefore I am told it does not exist.

My reputation as a difficult patient precedes me. Along with chronic pain and recurrent infection, I now have a psychiatric history. In many doctors' eyes, I have no credibility.

When Trevor gets home from work, we sit together at the end of the couch, in the dark closeness of late evening.

"I want to give the surgeon the benefit of the doubt," I say.

"He sewed us up and has been so caring and supportive. I want to keep him on my side." I push myself under Trevor's arm. His prickly beard irritates the skin on the left side of my face. "I can't go back to the doctors who did the prosthesis. They say the bolts are inert. What do I do now?"

His hand squeezes my shoulder. "It would make such a difference to your depressions to have you well. We need to fight!"

We sit without speaking for a minute. "What about seeing someone new?" I ask.

We run through the names of doctors we know and come up with a former classmate of Trevor's, Jake Richards. He works at the hospital in Calgary. Trevor agrees to call him.

I look across the room at the soft pastels of the print on the wall. It shows an angel cradling a small child.

Jake Richards is dark-haired and heavyset, with a habit of twirling his glasses. Trevor and I had made the trip to Calgary when my infection flared yet again, and I have spent the last week and a half on intravenous antibiotics to get it under control. I am still in my hospital bed, Trevor perched nervously beside me. We have rehearsed how to present our story and our desire for surgical investigation, and we are comforted somewhat when the young surgeon appears happy to see us. We catch up on each other's lives; work and new houses and children.

"So, you've asked for a consult. How can I help?"

Trevor and I fill in the history, beginning with the infections in New Zealand, and I describe the lump in my cheek. Dr. Richards is shaking his head, and he has even taken a step back from us as we speak. I feel desperation rising in me but know I must disguise the intensity of my need. I've learned nothing scares a doctor away faster.

"We wondered, could you look at the screw sites?" I say carefully. "Would you be willing to check under the new cheekbone? Just to see if there is any sign of abscess?"

Trevor continues. "If there's pus or dead bone in there, the infection will keep flaring up until that's cleaned out. Antibiotics don't seem to be the answer. We have to try something else."

Jake peers at Trevor, then at me. "I don't know. I don't think I can help. Things have settled right down now, and your face looks great. Go home and take it easy. You'll be fine."

"Jake, we've been through this movie too many times," Trevor says. "The infection is not going away, and it's eight hours of driving to come back every time it returns. It's kicking the stuffing out of us. We're just asking you to open things up and have a look. That's all. I don't want to plead, but I guess that's what I'm doing."

Jake turns to go. "I'll think about it."

The next day the antibiotics are completed, and tomorrow I will be sent home. Jake is still not convinced.

"Please," we ask him on his rounds. "Please, even a tiny look."

He sighs. "All right. Those screws would take a jackhammer to remove. No one will touch them. But I can look under the rib graft. I'll see what I can do. I'll schedule a surgery as soon as I can."

Post-operatively, I am groggy and anxious. We must wait until the end of Dr. Richards' busy day to get a report. When he finally enters the room, he moves confidently towards us.

"You'll never guess what I found," he says. "There was an abscess behind your rib graft, the size of a golf ball. We had to clean it all out. We were right. It's a good thing we went looking." He seems proud, and I am torn with emotion. Delight and hope mingle with the urge to throw something at him, and at all those other doctors. Almost three years! And even then we had to beg.

❦

I am pregnant again.

I have lost what would have been our fourth child already, at twenty weeks' gestation. We named him Theo. Theodore. Beloved of God. He was perfectly formed. Did my medications kill him? Did the infections make it impossible for him to live inside me?

This recent pregnancy has arrived against all odds, and I believe this little one is meant to be with us. Daniel pipes up at the supper table, Trevor shushing Ellen's singing so that we can hear him clearly: "Mommy, do you know what I think? I think this baby is Theo. He really wants to be in our family. So he is trying again. He wants to get born." But as my abdomen grows, so does my anguish.

For eight months after the abscess was drained, I had blessed relief from infection, and the face pain markedly improved. But it has been steadily increasing in intensity for several months now, and I have periodic flare-ups of swelling, redness and fever. Depression lives with me, my dark shadow. I am hospitalized again at Hills Pavilion, with a protuberant stomach. When I am too big to curl up anymore, I lie straight with my hands covering my face. IV antibiotics pump into my arm. I don't want anyone to see me. I fantasize about dying, being gone.

Most mornings I don't want to leave my room. I don't get dressed until the nurse hassles me, and then it takes forever. I'm long past caring whether or not my hair is brushed or my teeth are clean. The psychiatrist comes to see me in my room. His woolly jacket and tie are crisp and clean, his face neatly shaved. I crave his approval. The smile in his eyes when he says hello means more to me than he will ever know.

"Trish, I don't think you're ready to go home yet. I'm concerned about your impulsiveness when you get low and agitated. Your last time home you took a pretty hefty dose of your pills. There's a biological basis here, and I'm optimistic the medications we're giving you this time around might make a difference."

"I am afraid," I say, my eyes fixed on the creases in his pants.

"What are you afraid of?"

I am quiet a moment, wondering whether to risk telling him. "I am afraid you'll get sick of me."

He laughs. "Trish, I've got a lot invested in you. I'm not about to give up." He uncrosses his legs, and I am scared he is getting up to leave. I catch his eye, beseeching.

"You are a very powerful person," he says. "I feel it even when you are down. You are a threat to others with your horrible experiences and the complexity of your feelings. That's why some of the staff here have trouble dealing with you. Your suffering runs deep." He stands. "We'll get you through this tough time bit by bit. Keep you and your baby safe."

When he is gone, I wrap my arms around my belly. "Hey, my baby," I croon. "Don't die. Don't have anything wrong with you."

The nurse, earlier this morning, wanted me to recite some affirmations. I remember two: I am lovable and capable. I have a source of inner contentment. As I say these in my head, over and over, I begin to shake from head to toe. Faces float before me. Smiling. Sweet. Then people with axes and knives. Chopping. Slashing. Blood everywhere.

The crying comes jagged and gut-wrenching. I rock violently on the bed, my breathing growing shallower and shallower until I am lightheaded.

The nurse is sharp and tells me to stop it. I ask her to sit with me, but she brings medication. After a long, long while the body movements stop and I am still, deadened again. Sedated.

In sleep, I dream. I sit with my pills in their little brown containers. The bear is there beside me, and she grabs the pills from me. Her five-inch claws are like fingers, supple and quick, as she opens the bottles and takes my medicine. "Hey," I want to say, "those are mine. Don't take so many. They could be dangerous." But I am too afraid to speak. She rolls on her side, smiling as she falls asleep with the pills clenched tightly in her paws. I am restless, agitated, but I must stay very still. I must not wake the bear.

Trevor wants to care for me at home. He is afraid the psych ward is too unloving a place. He negotiates with the psychiatrist for me to continue ECT on an outpatient basis; it is the only thing that pulls me back even a little from catatonia and suicidal thoughts. Every Monday, Wednesday and Friday, at six-thirty in the morning, he drives me to Hills Pavilion. He walks me, huddled and shuffling, into the hospital, then he and the children go for their breakfast of hash browns and sausage McMuffins at the drive-through. They spend an hour in the park by the river, playing on the swings or reading aloud from *The Blue Castle* under the giant old trees. When they return for me, I am drowsy and disoriented. I sleep in the back seat in a bed of blankets while Trevor drives us all home. He drops the children off at school, then tucks me into bed. Friends take the children sometimes, or bring dessert or lasagna. They ask how things are going, but they rarely want to hear the whole truth.

Trevor and I are both running on empty. No one knows what else to do for us. The staff at the Hills Pavilion talk of sending me to the Fraser Unit, a large psychiatric hospital, but I beg them no. I need to be with people who love me. I try to shape up, to snap out of it, but my efforts defeat me.

The pregnancy draws to a close. The children have helped me go through the boxes in the garage to find our baby things. We still have the little yellow quilt I bought for Nicola ten years ago. There are a few toys and bundles of tiny diapers. We won't have room in the apartment for the cradle that held the other children. Trevor has set up a travel-sized playpen in our bedroom, tucked under the sloping eaves.

My labour is silent, long and hard. At its midpoint, I see Trevor's chalk-white face and ask him if he shouldn't leave the room. The baby finally comes in two big pushes. A large, bald, screaming, red-faced boy. He is vigorous and strong. I cry with relief, exhausted, sweaty and grateful. There is no cleft lip and palate, no Down syndrome, no anomaly, nothing wrong. I pull him close, my arms weary already with his solid weight. He nurses eagerly. William. Will. "Resolute and brave."

We are inundated with gifts and cards. Neighbours and friends who have followed our saga pour their happiness for us into heartfelt messages. There are handmade quilts and tiny outfits, books with Will's name in the front. There are meals and cookies for us to put in the freezer for a rainy day. We are washed with the love of all these good wishes.

Still, I am weighted. I had hoped that after the birth my depression would leave me. I can pull myself up for hours at a time, come out of my bedroom to be with my family, but I feel as though I am on another planet. It is painfully lonely. I don't dare tell anyone about the nightmares of being chased and assaulted that torture me night and day. I nuzzle the fuzz on the baby's little head and try to fill myself with his goodness, his fresh smell, the hope he is made of.

The baby is three months old, and I cannot stop crying. I come home from two weeks in the hospital with another infection, and I cannot nurse Will anymore. Trevor has taken over, changing Will, holding, rocking and feeding him. My psychiatrist has stressed the importance of getting out of our small, crowded quarters, but building the big house is a huge task, and Trevor cannot keep up. He hires help with the plumbing and drywalling, and several times his father, Daun, comes to work with him.

When the veil lifts, even slightly, I make myself get up and out. I take Will to a mothers' group, feeling awkward with my scarred face and the years I have on the young mothers there. We sit like colourful flowers in a garden bed, fair and dark, thin and fat, in chairs around the circumference of the room. I am looking for communion with the other women, but their easy conversation and laughter is like a room I don't have a key to.

I am sent to Hills Pavilion again. I come home for a few weeks, then go back to the hospital. I am home for another month after that, determined I will take over my roles and cope. I practise affirmations, but home alone one day visions of atrocities leave me frenzied, shaking and sweating in our little bedroom. My knees are rubbed raw with the rhythmic movement of my legs on the bedclothes. Desperate to find calm, I take too many pills. The woman on the crisis line sends the police to my home. I am taken to emergency.

Trevor is at the breaking point. He takes me to Hills, but the staff send us home. Frightened by my talk of death, Trevor drives me back again. They admit me, but they are running out of patience and want to send me to a larger psych ward. They are tired of me. Everyone is. I am hurting Trevor. I am a terrible example for my children. I frighten my mother.

I am no good.

I cannot escape the physical pain in my head, the infections that have returned to plague me, the visions, the nightmares, the complete and utter despair. I know it would be better for everyone if I were gone. I will be doing them all a favour if I kill myself.

I try.

They send me away.

☙

From the beginning, the staff at the big city hospital, the Fraser Unit, treat me like a naughty child. Much later, I will learn they are practising behaviour modification. It feels like cruelty. I am chastised for lying on my bed, for being homesick, for being sad. They tell me to watch television to divert myself from the head pain and the agitation that comes with flashbacks. The nurse brings me stacks of magazines, suggesting that I rip them up to vent my anger. After five times saying no thank you, I throw them across the room. When I can't concentrate on the cognitive therapy workbook they bring me, they say my attitude is pathetic; I am not trying hard enough. I am told over and over that I am not here to deal with my "issues." One day when I thank a nurse for taking the time to sit and talk with me, she pulls away, angry; according to the staff, my happy gratitude means that I am trying to win her over to my side. I don't like the way I behave in response to the way they treat me. I fantasize about running away, hiding on the streets from the police they would send after me. I want to go home.

I was at Hills when I tried to kill myself. I had asked not to be left alone, but they did leave me alone. I paced, hit the bed, called out. The many-coloured pills were in my pocket. After, the world swam in dizzying circles. A loud rush entered my head, and I fell. I woke in the intensive care unit. Trevor was punctured, wounded in a way I had never seen before; my mother was sickened. I can't hurt them again, or my children. I am not allowed to die. In utter despair, I weep.

For the first month at the Fraser Unit, I am given ECT every second weekday. I have eleven sessions. My mind gets so thick that I can't remember the staff who cared for me the day before or what we talked about.

It is my birthday. Trevor visits, a ten-hour drive from Napier, bringing me an amethyst necklace and earrings. On his next visit, weeks later, I show him the necklace, curious about where such a beautiful thing could have come from. "Don't you remember?" he asks, then reaches for me. He reads me a love poem he has written. We are perched on the edge of my single bed, the curtains pulled on an overcast fall day. I am in my pyjamas; the staff has locked up my clothing to punish me for staying too long off the ward, even though I didn't know there was a time limit. In my hand is a cluster of notes I've written for Trevor to take back to our children. They are full of an optimism I don't feel, a love I am desperate to communicate.

For a while they called me manic depressive. I liked that label. It took the responsibility away from me. Since then, I have been diagnosed with a major depressive disorder, symptoms of personality disorder, and an adjustment disorder. Apparently that means I am sad and manipulative and dependent and avoidant and not good at coping with having bad things happen to me. I *am* all those things. I crave acceptance and love from the hospital staff; that would unleash my pain, allow me to get past the suffering. But it seems they are afraid they will be succumbing to manipulation if they offer me support.

The hospital does a psychological assessment to ascertain whether I am suffering from post-traumatic stress disorder. There are six criteria for PTSD, the interviewer tells me. Following a traumatic event in which the person fears death or injury, he or she experiences persistent feelings of horror or helplessness. Nightmares, intrusive thoughts, a reduced interest in others, agitation, irritability and outburts of rage are common. The interviewer reads the criteria to me from the *DSM-IV*, the fat blue book psychiatrists use for diagnosis. I sit unmoving, feeling as though she and I are talking about someone else.

The report comes back from Psychology at the end of the week, indicating that I meet the diagnostic criteria for PTSD. A staff person files it away in my chart.

The faces, pure and sweet, float through the air towards me. As they get closer, they twist and contort in agony. They are hideous: cut, bloody, in pieces. Even with my eye open, they keep coming at me. I bang my head on the wall. I need help, but I am afraid to tell the staff. They will be angry, tell me to deal with it myself.

My roommate, Barb, is a soft, grey-haired woman, a psychiatric nurse when she is well. Her arms go around me, and she hugs me tight.

"Hey," she says. "What's going on? Trish. Hey." I sob uncontrollably. "I'm going to get a nurse."

When she comes back, she sits beside me, her arm around my shoulder. She tries to calm me. Bloody faces, dark red and black, rise in front of me over and over again.

"The nurses said to leave you alone," Barb says angrily. "I can't do that. You need someone with you." She leans over, tries to pull me upright. "Sit up. Let me hold you. Open your eyes."

"Oh God. Make them go away!"

"Open your eyes."

She leaves the room again, and when she returns she is furious. "I'm being moved. We're not roommates anymore. I'm not supposed to help you. You're supposed to tough it out alone. Damn, I hate this place."

Two nurses enter. Their backs to me, they instruct Barb to bundle up her belongings. Then she is gone.

I am awake long hours. When I finally sleep, I dream I am in the ECT room. The smell of medication is in the air. Nurses and a doctor move around me, expressionless and silent; I am naked, cold in the thin blue gown. I am frightened. No one looks at me, though I cast my glance about. The doctor holds the oxygen mask over my head and begins to lower it. It is heavy and black and smells of rubber. A hand pins my resisting arm to the table. Another hand presses down on my shoulder. The mask comes lower and I squirm, frantically trying to get away. It is the bear's mouth that they are putting over my face! I fight. Hands push me down, hold the mask firmly in place. The bear begins to chew, eating out the middle of my face. Horrifying noise, of bones breaking. Smell of thick bear fur, horrible bear breath. The taste of anaesthetic rises in my throat and I am sinking, sinking, sinking away.

When I awake from the anaesthetic, I am crying. The nurses tell me to stop. I try. I don't want them to be angry with me.

I have asked for a plastic surgery consultation while I'm here. I want to see a new specialist about my face pain and infections. A pustule has opened in a reddened area under my eye patch. I am petrified of presenting myself to yet another doctor, but this may be my last chance. I need a solution, an answer, and I am still suspicious about the titanium bolts in my left brow.

My Vancouver friend Laura, her face lit with life under a cap of red hair, accompanies me to Dr. Donnelly's office. She is optimistic because she doesn't know any better. I am sick with anxiety. What if the doctor won't listen? What if he says I just have to keep living with the pain?

Dr. Donnelly is attentive as he examines me and reads the one-page history I have prepared. He looks directly at me, asking questions and listening carefully to my story. I am overwhelmed by his kindness. I have become used to thinking that my feelings don't count. "It's incredible what you've been through," he says finally. "Let's take those bolts out of there." I sit stunned, ecstatic, as he books a scan and a surgery for the end of the week.

Back on the ward, I tell my nurse, with a tentative smile, what the plan is. With no response, she turns away.

I am supposed to be discharged after the surgery. I was told once before that I was ready to go home, but at the last minute they called in a new psychiatrist and recommitted me. Not much has changed in the two months I've been here, except that I feel wounded to the core, and, somewhere deep inside, very angry.

One night I dream the psychiatrist from the Fraser Unit is at my house. His intense blue eyes follow me as I run from room to room, gathering my children around me like a frantic hen. He is after us. He wants to hurt us. Without warning he throws a blanket over us like a net. We wrap our arms around each other, crying. He begins tearing at the net, biting and clawing. My children scream. I fight to cover them with my body, to take the attack myself.

I jerk awake, filmed with sweat. I long for comfort and reassurance, but I don't dare approach anyone.

The next day is a bad one. My legs and arms tremble. The twisted, bloody faces loom. By late evening, I am sorely frightened. I feel like hurting myself. No pills to take, yet I'm terrified of being alone. Out to the seating area next to the nursing station. Sit. Everyone else is in bed. Visions circle. Teeth. Blood. Faces. I'm truly losing it this time. Fear burrows in.

At the nurses' desk. Tentative. "Can you help me?" Push myself against the wall.

She's reading a newspaper and hardly looks up. Speaks sharply. "Go to bed. Now."

Recoil. How to make her see? Try again. Terror of her, but worse of myself. My promise to Trevor and my mother that I will not hurt myself again, will ask for help when I need it.

"Please. I'm in trouble." Choke it out.

Her head snaps up and she shouts, one arm stabbing in fury towards my room. "Stop this nonsense right now. Get your pyjamas on and go to bed."

Hard against the wall. Spiralling uncertainty. Thoughts racing. Visions, voices, screaming. Want to hit the wall, smash it out, get thinking away. Doors are open, down the outer hallway. Must find someone. Out the door. Running on bare feet, find an exit, and out. The emergency department. Receptionist. I am shaking, incoherent, bent over my lap and sobbing. She leans forward on her desk, harsh. "What do you want?" Try to ask for someone. Someone to be with me in this. I make no sense. She is leaning, fierce, yelling. "What do you want?" She pulls back, reaching for the phone, her voice loud. "I'm going to call security." My hair on end, clothes awry, body bulky, sobbing, shaking. Security? No! They will take me back to the unit. They will be angry. Why is she yelling? I yell too. How do I stop this nightmare? What have I done?

The security guards arrive. I shrivel. One on each side, they hold my arms. They are soft-spoken, their hands gentle. I am dishevelled and shaking, but inside, their caring soothes, comforts, quiets me. My head droops.

The nurse at the ward desk is waiting and furious. "What do you think you're doing? Take these pills right now, or I'll hold you down and give you a shot. Get your pyjamas on. You're going into seclusion."

Panic. I pull at the arms restraining me. "No!" I shout. Afraid.

Down another long hallway, a guard on either side. A heavy door with one small window. Unlocked, and I am ushered inside. Square room. Stainless-steel toilet, mattress, blanket. "Please, don't lock me up alone in here." I lean against the wall, clawing at it with my hands. "I want to go home. I want my family."

The nurse's voice is suddenly calm. "I'll bring you more medication later."

Weeping, I fold myself in my own arms. The nurse and guards turn to leave, pulling shut and then locking the solid expanse of door behind them.

It is morning. There is no outside window to tell me so, but an entourage arrives: the psychiatry resident, a medical student, a nurse and three security guards. They tell me through a little slit in the door to stay seated on the floor while they enter. I sit, flat and dead. They tower above me.

Have I calmed down? Yes. Will I behave on the unit? Yes. Do I feel suicidal? No. I'm fine, I'm obedient, I'll be good, just let me out of here. I move mechanically, wondering why they need six people to escort me back to the unit. Once we get there, everyone disperses. I am told to eat my breakfast. That's it. The end. Life goes on now.

I am quiet for the next few days. I fear they might call off my surgery if I misbehave. The other patients are indignant, full of their own stories of angry staff and seclusion. They counsel me in the sitting area.

"Trish," says Barb, "you've got to be a good patient if you want to get out of here."

Rolf has been suicidal since losing his partner. "You have to play the game their way," he says. "Make them think they're getting somewhere. Make them feel successful."

"They keep committing you, and you get worse if you stay," Lucy adds. She is fragile-looking, dressed in ill-fitting clothes. "Don't do anything to upset them."

I am dismayed. "But how can we pretend to be fine when we're not? We shouldn't be lying about how we feel."

Barb shakes her head. "Nobody's going to get better in here. This is just a holding tank."

The surgery is successful. The intravenous has to be started in my neck because my arm and foot sites are all used up. The operating-room staff are wonderfully humane, asking me beforehand about my apprehensions, laughing at my request to have Trevor faxed here to be with me. When I wake in the recovery room, I struggle to talk through the grogginess. "Did he take the screws out?" Yes, the screws are out. I cry and cry, washed with hope and relief.

Dr. Donnelly calls me several days later with the details. The third bolt lifted right out without him having to drill it, he says. The bone around it was mushy. The silicone implant in my left temple was infected, and he removed that as well.

My psychiatrist and his medical resident are standing by the office when I get off the phone. Wreathed in smiles, I tell them my news. They look at me expressionless. But my friends, the other patients, share in my rejoicing.

No, I don't feel suicidal, I tell the doctor a few days later. Yes, I feel ready to go home. Yes, my time here has been very helpful.

I am free. Trevor comes to take me home. I have been away for ten weeks. Fifteen years ago this month, Trevor and I were discharged from hospital following the bear attack.

❧

Summer has turned to fall. Our little town is saturated in yellows and oranges. The trees branch over my head as I walk. Walking is supposed to release endorphins, make me feel better. I skid on the chestnuts lying thick underfoot.

I am escaping my home, the love I feel I don't deserve, the needs I feel I cannot meet. I don't belong there; they have learned to live without me. The days seem endless. I crave disappearing, sleep, death. Inside me is a dark fear that this is who I will always be.

Since my time on the Fraser Unit, anger consumes me, chokes me, overwhelms me. Did they truly mean to help me with their "care"? I am enraged by my treatment there.

I have regular appointments with a counsellor at the Mental Health office downtown, but I don't know if there is any point to talking with anyone about all this. I keep circling around the same issues and saying the same things. More than anything, I need to let out the sadness, the anger, the grief. When I tried to do that in the hospital, I was medicated, shamed, even locked up. Where else can I go? Certainly not to the Mental Health office, with its manicured carpets and staff all dressed just so. How could I scream the screams I hear? How could I howl out my rage at the years of infections until the screws were finally pulled? How could I cry from the depths of my wailing heart and not scare everyone in the building?

Trevor has hired a nanny, and I think about ways to ease myself back into home life. My counsellor tells me about a halfway house, a place for people who need a bridge from the hospital back into the community. I go to see it, but it's just another psych ward in miniature. I rent the upstairs of an old house instead. It has a tiny kitchenette and bathroom, room for a bed and a desk. Trevor helps me move over the essentials. He insists I take the computer, in case I want to write.

I keep the room for six months. Sometimes I stay there for days and nights at a time, when I am particularly low and can't stand to let my family see me. I lie and look at the sloped ceiling for hours, sorting through the emotions each day brings. I take pills and sleep. Trevor and I have an agreement that I will not hurt myself, that I will tell someone or go to hospital if I am in trouble. He comes to visit. We make coffee and eat pastries and sit in the light from the small dormer window on the east wall. We lie together on the bed, arms and legs entangled.

I love having my little place. The visions and the sadness colour my days, but in the quiet hours I begin to come alive again. A small self is awakening within.

One weekend I am home with the kids while Trevor is on call. In the middle of the night, Ellen comes to my bedside. I slide over, arms wide open, and hold up the covers for her. She climbs in and lies close, gazing at my unpatched eye. She brings her snub nose right up against mine and pushes gently.

"Hi, Mom."

"Ellen, time to sleep. Just cuddle."

"You're not going to die?"

"Only when I'm old. Shhh."

She sucks her thumb quietly for a moment. Squinting my eye

open I see her wide blue-eyed gaze. "Your eye that's gone, doesn't it hurt you?"

"Sometimes."

"I've got a loose tooth."

"Shhh."

"A bear won't get me, right?"

"No. I won't let it."

Her breathing slows. She murmurs, then brings a chubby finger up to my face.

"I see your light."

"What light?" I am puzzled.

"Your light. You're beautiful, Mom."

Her limbs go soft. I gaze at the profusion of freckles marching across her fresh little face and the thick line of lashes fringing her eyes. I bring my head forward to nuzzle the mess of hair, tightening my arms around her still, heavy form.

But though I have moments when the cloud engulfing me seems to lift, I can't sustain the feeling.

I crash terribly several times. Back at Hills Pavilion, the staff can't or won't forgive my suicide attempt. I want to understand what happened that day, but they won't discuss it. My doctor is different with me, and many of the nurses are offhand and distant. They want to manipulate me into being a repentant patient. In turn, I become manipulative of them, constantly seeking attention. When my family doctor and my counsellor tell me of a local psychiatrist, Dr. King, I reluctantly agree to see him. I have a secret plan this time, though. I will not trust the doctor. I will guard myself. He will not get in.

Dr. King is a big man, polite, with a strong, welcoming handshake. He speaks in a courteous, attentive voice, telling me first about himself and his philosophies, then about his desire to help me take charge of what is going on.

"I don't want to tell my story again," I mumble, head down.

"I would be honoured if you would share it with me," he says.

I tell him a little piece. About the bear attack. About wanting to be dead. He and I both know there is much more. But my stomach is clenching, and my hands are beginning to shake. He is quiet a moment, then reaches to the shelf behind him for a large book.

"Have you ever heard of post-traumatic stress disorder?" he asks, flipping through the pages.

"Yes. They added that to my list of diagnoses at the Fraser Unit."

"Well, here. Read this."

I read. I focus as I could not in the hospital.

"It's me exactly." I lift my face to look at him. "The dreams, isolating myself, the agitation."

"Let's get rid of all those other labels," Dr. King says firmly. "PTSD's still a relatively new diagnosis. There isn't a great deal known about it, and treatment is not well defined. I will see you at the local hospital when you need to be hospitalized. We don't have a psych ward, but the nurses can care for you just fine. Come through emergency and tell them to let me know when you are admitted. I want you to make the choices, take back some control of your life."

I nod. Despite myself, I feel hopeful.

I am admitted to our local hospital several times, rocking with profound unrest or sunk in despair. Usually I have stopped eating and drinking, and it can take up to nine pokes to start the IV on my overused veins. The emergency department doctors who admit me are Trevor's colleagues and friends.

One night the hospital is full. The unit clerk does some juggling to get me a space so I will not have to spend the night on a stretcher in emergency. In the noisy four-bed ward I am wheeled to hours later, it is potluck which nurses I get. Some concentrate completely on physical care, whisking me about as though I were the dead blob I am. Others spend time with me.

I hand over my pills to one of the nurses. My agitation is fearful, and I am frightened I will be sent to Hills. Dr. King comes to see me late in the evening. "Trish, you're not going back to the psych ward if you don't want to go."

"How do I get through this? What should I do when I'm really losing it?" My body shakes with large tremors.

He places his hand on my shoulder. "There is no cure, but the medication will help."

"As soon as I start to relax, I'm afraid I'm going to fall. I jerk and catch myself."

"It's part of it. Part of PTSD." His voice rumbles through my anxiety like a steamroller. "Allow yourself to feel whatever you're feeling. Accept it. Just be."

The next nurse who comes in has a flannel fresh from the warming cupboard and a cup of camomile tea. She wraps me in a blanket and pulls her chair close. She asks me not to give up.

Trevor visits during his on-call shift in emergency. He adjusts my intravenous rate, then crawls onto the bed beside me, his beeper's hard edge against my hip. He sings quietly as his warm hand cradles the scarred side of my face.

After he leaves, I dream I am lying on a mountainside. It is night, and the sky above me is peppered with stars. I find Ursa Major and search out the bear's shape, knowing the legends of those who were banished from the earth to become eternal bears. Suddenly the land pushes me away and up and I am propelled into the black sky. The bear encompasses me, stifling my breathing, deadening my limbs. I struggle to get away.

I awake with a gasp and turn the light on, trying to erase the cold desolation of that night sky. When the tears come, I go with them, into despair and grief, and at the end peace fills me. Comforted, I sleep.

My counsellor comes with the morning sun. Light bounces around the room, and I find I am smiling at her. The dark has left me. I am back again.

My anger at the Fraser Unit staff is energizing me in a way I couldn't have imagined. I am filled with indignation that some-one so crushed could be treated so poorly, so cruelly. I see now that I have been treating myself unkindly as well. I must start to speak up, defend myself, take charge.

The final week in my little apartment, I type a letter of com-plaint to the Fraser Unit. That is what their human relations department has suggested I do. They've assured me a thorough investigation will be made of my concerns. When the letter is sent off, I feel a great release.

I pack my little apartment into boxes and cart them home. Home is the big house now. Trevor has finished varnishing two thousand square feet of flooring, and everything is ready for us to move in.

Morning light pours into the kitchen, across wood counters and white cabinets. Late in the day, light spills over the patterned carpet we bought so many years ago with this living room in mind. Upstairs, the same glorious light fills our bedroom, falling in at the French windows.

Best of all, for the first time in my life, I have a room of my own. It is tiny, with a little swing-out window looking onto the lake. By the door, Trevor has made a built-in desk and shelving unit that houses my books, my files, my miniature figurines and my computer. Now I will write.

I'm reading in bed one evening when Trevor comes up our back hill during a break from his night shift in emergency. He's in good spirits, but he has sat with me less than five minutes when he is called in again for a patient suffering from anxiety.

"Oh," he says, sliding into his shoes, "I forgot to tell you. I just about stepped on a bear on the trail through the lot behind our house."

"What?!" I ask, sitting up straight. "When?"

"Just now." He is laughing, pulling a sweater over his head. "It's pitch-black out there. Suddenly there was this dark shape right in front of me that went crashing off through the underbrush. Surprised the living daylights out of both of us."

"So you're going to walk the long way around this time?"

He's almost out the bedroom door. Clumping down the wooden stairs, he yells back. "Don't worry. I scared it. It's halfway to Vancouver by now."

I pick up my book, but my concentration is broken. I keep imagining the bulk and the noise of the bear in the dark.

One afternoon I have a date with Ellen and Nicola. Downtown feels like a carnival. The blooming magnolia trees, planters of tulip blossoms, street musicians playing guitar, harp and violin put magic in the air. It is a day for ice-cream cones and sitting on a bench to watch the world go by.

We stand at a street corner waiting for the light to change. Nicola is almost as tall as I am now, her high cheekbones showing off clear eyes that sweep the busy streets around us, constantly appraising. She looks so much like I used to. Ellen dresses herself these days, and she is wearing pink and red and green: sweatpants, a floral skirt, a star-covered sweater. She cut her own hair this morning and has no bangs anymore.

I thought I had given up on perfection, but I am self-conscious as I stand there on the curb. My body is trimmer and carefully dressed today, but still I am alert to staring and dread the thought of questions about my face. I crave normalcy, whatever that might be.

The elderly woman waiting next to us looks over. I look away, hoping she will not ask about the patch. She is about to say something when Ellen saves the day. "You have wrinkles," she says to the woman. Everyone laughs. The light changes and we are on our way.

At the clothing store, Nicola and I show each other silk suits and embroidered sweater sets. Laughing like girlfriends, we try on whatever we like while Ellen stands in front of the full-length mirror, making faces and talking to herself.

We stop to get a drink after our shopping. The woman behind the counter in the coffee shop recognizes me. She's heard about the attack.

"My husband and I saw a bear in the woods last weekend," she says. "He wanted to finish our hike anyway. What do you think we should have done?"

I shake my head. I don't collect bear stories, I want to tell her. I'm not an expert. But I just ask her for a decaf latte instead.

On the bus home, Ellen makes her unsteady way to the very

back. I sit beside Nicola, leaning my head against the window.
From behind us comes Ellen's unmistakable voice, full volume,
singing with a vengeance to a tune of her own.

The bear got Mom and the bear got Dad
Mommy got bit on the eye
And she cried
Daddy didn't cry
And Mommy climbed a tree
She fell down
Bear can't get me . . .

Nicola groans. I start to get up, to retrieve Ellen, to stop her.
But what does it matter? I'm enjoying watching the neat little
houses going by, the lovely new green of the trees. I massage the
left side of my face where it aches, hold Nicola's hand and laugh.

With Oenone, our nanny, here to help around the house, I can
break my days into manageable pieces. I am coming back to
earth, reclaiming the soul I abandoned long ago. I spend time
with each of my children, savouring their love as the most powerful medicine of all. I can rest when I want, though since the
removal of the bolts and the infection I am free of cellulitis.
Without hospitalizations and surgeries, the nightmares and
visions torment me less. I take time each day to write, read, sleep

or just think, looking at the trembling aspens outside my bedroom window for hours. I thrive on my time alone. The respect
and support of the staff at our local hospital have helped lighten
the shame that has weighed me down for so long. The Fraser
Unit responds to my complaint, calling my care there "excel-
lent," and for a time I feel searing anger. But I refuse to live in
bitterness and resentment. I send them framed prints of my
favourite quotes as a gesture of reconciliation and find that it
soothes the burn. I call some local mental-health organizations,
offering to speak to their staff people about my experience. Maybe that will change things for other patients.

A therapist with a large heart and lots of patience does body-
work, craniosacral work and acupuncture with me, giving me an
outlet for strong emotion. I am dropping almost ten pounds a
month as I come off the alphabet soup of drugs I was prescribed.
Our new house is starting to be the loving nest I had hoped for.
The low periods still come, but they are not as intense or as
frequent.

Life is exhilarating when I am well. Colours and textures and
tastes delight me once again, and I wear my children's laughter
like a crown. When Trevor and I walk downtown for a date I
want to swing hands, hug on the street and sit for hours in my
favourite tearoom with the mismatched chairs and dishes. Even
if it is cloudy or raining, I am soaked in light.

The more my life comes into balance, though, the more I

notice Trevor struggling. He is slower and quieter, and he hasn't worked on the house for months. The spark that usually shines so brilliantly in him now glows dimly. He can cope when I am depressed, but when I am doing well his feet drag and life is an effort. He is often short-tempered.

One afternoon we spill into our big front entryway after a family walk in the country, knapsacks, coats, hats, mitts and boots spreading everywhere. My mother is with us, spending a week visiting.

Trevor disappears upstairs to change Will, and I head into the kitchen to turn on the burner under our supper of chicken soup. On my way past, I push the message button on the answering machine.

"Dr. Janz. Please call the hospital when you get in."

Beep.

"Nicola. Hi. It's Keira. Have you started that book yet? Call me when you get in."

Beep.

"Trevor." The caller is Trevor's sister Margot. She's crying. "Trevor. Please call Canmore. Mama's died."

In a daze, I head upstairs, where I can hear Trevor singing. How am I going to tell him?

We finish the day in slow motion. Hushed voices and many tears. We pack up the truck for the trip to Alberta.

The funeral is huge. Afterward, dozens of people fill the beautiful home in Canmore. Everything speaks of Sarah. The sweaters people are wearing. The table linens. The artwork on the walls. There are bits of her everywhere, but she is gone.

Over the next few weeks, Trevor sinks even lower into himself. He doesn't want to answer the phone or leave the house. He hauls himself off to work, looking dead tired. He lies on the bed for hours during the day, but at night is up and wandering. My depression returns, and I have to be hospitalized. Trevor stifles his own grief to support me yet again, to be fully present at work and for the children.

It is a thin veneer of managing, and holding it together drives him into a corner. Things are strained between us once I'm home. I can't reach Trevor; he is withdrawn and silent. One night as I lie in our room waiting for him, he comes to the foot of the bed.

"I never promised I would always love you and support you."

I can't believe what I am hearing. I will him to look my way, but he is removing his clothes, concentrating on the slow unbuttoning of his shirt.

"You did! *We* did. What were our vows about?"

"I never promised that I would love you forever."

When he climbs into bed, he stays carefully to one side. "I can't promise you anything, Trish. I don't know anymore."

I feel as if the bed is dropping out from under me. "Trevor. What about growing old and wrinkly together?"

He doesn't respond. I want to hit him, to yell at him to come back, not to give up on us. But I see his despair and know I can ask for nothing. He has nurtured me through surgeries, infections, pain and depression after depression. His love has fed my soul, my beliefs, my will to try. Now that is what I can offer him.

"No matter what, I love you," I say. I send it out into the darkened room.

Week after week, Trevor sees patients who have come to emergency with broken bones or back pain or anxiety. He opens himself to them, takes on extra shifts. He spends long hours with the children, telling stories to the three youngest and taking all the kids out on the lake for days at a time in our sailboat. But he has no desire to work on the house, and he often shuts himself away to lie on our bed and pray or read his philosophy books.

He is polite with me but not affectionate. When I try to embrace him, his body does not respond. I can't lean on his solidity anymore. I yearn for an "I love you" to plug the stream of insecurity washing through me. I used to think I knew what it was to feel alone.

One evening we are peeling vegetables for supper. I watch my hands, seeing where I have bitten my nails to the quick.

"I've never been so tired." Trevor's voice is quiet. I hold my breath lest I break the spell, the carrot scraper stilled. "I can't keep up." I risk glancing sideways, see his head bent forward. "Trish, I'm scared. Nothing feels the same." He looks over at me.

I look back, still afraid to speak. "I miss my mother so much."

I reach for his hand and hold it, kiss it, until he turns away. The sound of the viola he is teaching himself to play comes from behind closed doors as I finish preparing supper.

It is midnight, and Trevor has not come to bed. I find him sitting in the dark in the rocking chair, a sleeping Will in his arms. Once we're both in bed I pull on him, resisting his impulse to turn his back to me. Finally he gives in, burrowing his head into my shoulder and neck, and I wrap my arms around him. I hold him as I would one of the children. I smooth his hair, kiss his forehead and stroke his cheeks as he cries himself into exhaustion. That night I dream that the bear has got Trevor by the back of the neck. She is throwing him back and forth like a rag doll.

One evening, settled at my computer, I hear crying from down the hall. It is my first day back from the hospital after another low period. Daniel often reacts this way; he holds everything together when I am down, then falls apart when I come home. I go to his room, where he is wrapped cocoonlike in his panda comforter, lying sideways on the bed. His sobs are heart-wrenching.

"Ah, Daniel. What is it?"

"I don't know."

"What can I do for you?" I reach under the tightly wound bedding to rub his back.

While I was in the hospital, Daniel came down the hill with

an early crocus in a jar for me. I worry about what my depressions are doing to the kids, but his eyes held no judgement or blame. A smile split his freckled face, and the embrace he offered took my breath away. He knelt on the hospital bed, bouncing up and down, his face aglow. "I have something to tell you about, Mom. In a magazine it said they found a thing that can take away depression. It's chocolate, Mom. You just have to eat chocolate."

I think of this visit now as Daniel's sobs continue. I fight the tiredness I feel at the end of a long day.

"Daniel. This is getting to be too much. I don't know what to do. I'm frustrated."

His head struggles out from under the pillows. "Mommy." His eyes snap. "Maybe you don't have to do anything. Maybe I just need to cry. I want you to hold me."

I laugh a little, inside. I have felt this way so many times myself. I reach out in the darkness and enfold him, close to my heart.

Trevor is in bed when I get there, a shadow in the darkness.

"Is Daniel asleep?" he asks.

"Soundly. He was full of tears tonight."

"You know, I don't feel like doing paperwork or jobs around the house tomorrow. I think I'll go sailing. Will you come? The kids and I would like it."

I think of the effort it takes to still my panic when I am on the water. "You want me to? Sure, I'll come." I hope my voice sounds chipper enough.

For a moment there is only Trevor's breathing. "Can you be patient with me, Trish?"

"I'm trying."

"Is it all right if I only tell you I love you when I really mean it?" he asks.

"Is it all right if I don't act to please you, if I just be who I am?" I ask.

Outside our window, the clouds move away from a round, full moon, filling the room with soft light.

"Trish?"

"Yes?"

"I do love you."

"And I think I'll just stay home tomorrow. Not go sailing."

Elephant Mountain is on the other side of our local lake. Our plan is to climb to Candle Rock, partway up, and look back over the lake to town. The hike feels mystical today, with low cloud sitting in wisps all through the evergreens. The needles on the trees are such a dark green they are almost black.

The yellow rainsuits of the other children, the blue jacket of Nicola's friend, and the bright red of Trevor's anorak and rain pants are in bright contrast to the grey day as we start up the trail in a clump. Ellen hangs off my hand, complaining about the uphill climb. She hates to exert herself. I try to entice her with the promise of the view at the top and a snack.

"Are there chips?" she asks hopefully.

"No. Cookies."

"I want chips." She whines, shuffling beside me.

We've fallen behind, and the voices of the others are no longer audible. Abruptly, I am afraid. A friend told us last week of seeing a grizzly on the access road when he was cycling here. Couldn't have been a grizzly, I reassure myself. They wouldn't come this close to town. Just a black bear. Hah! When black bears attack, it's usually because they want to eat you. At least grizzlies are only defending themselves.

My eye combs the woods, tall maples devoid of leaves and sombre pines. Ellen throws the long stick she was carrying into the brush, and I jump at the sound. I try to stay calm. We are two people. We're making noise. The group ahead would have scared any bears away, right?

"Ellen. Let's sing," I suggest.

"Don't want to sing. Want to go home." She is sulky.

"Come on. Let's do Dona Nobis Pacem. You learned it at school. Remember?" I begin singing, loud and gutsy. Ellen shrieks in complaint and stops walking. I carry on slowly, singing the Latin line over and over. Then, remembering it means "give us peace," I change the words. "Give me peace in the woods," I sing. "Go away, bears. Give us peace in the woods."

Ellen's sullen look lifts as she hears me singing to the bears. She joins in eagerly. When a young couple with little bear bells on their daypacks come up behind us, we stand to the side to let them pass. I stifle my laughter at the embarrassed look on their faces. "What weirdos!" they seem to be thinking.

Ellen and I start our slow trudge once more, our voices strong as the tinkle of the hikers' silver bells vanishes in the mist.

VI

The Bear's Embrace

laintive and eerie, the long, strung-out notes fill my sister's living room. "It's called trance," John informs us happily, the rings in his lip moving as he speaks. He's six foot three at age fifteen. His hair, cropped short, has a purple hue. I remember seeing my enormously pregnant sister Margaret beside my hospital bed after the bear mauling all those years ago and wondering who the new baby would be. Here he is.

"You can't really call it music," my mother says from the easy chair, the light deepening the wrinkles on her face. "Can you?"

"It's great!" John's friend Eric exclaims. He and John launch excitedly into a discussion of the weekend's upcoming party.

It's the first time in a year that I've visited Margaret's house and caught up on the antics of her four boys. Even her thirteen-year-old is nearly six feet tall. Her oldest son has just moved out. As we sit drinking our coffee, John complains loudly, "I can't go anywhere. Everyone stares at me. They treat me rudely."

I laugh. "You've made the choice to look different. I'll trade you places. You take the permanent-looking different, and I'll have the earrings and coloured hair for a while."

I have come on this trip alone, to spend some time with my mother, sisters and brothers. I needed to spend some time in our childhood home, too. The old house is up for sale. My mother will find a smaller place without a mammoth yard and six empty bedrooms to rattle around in.

The shelves and cupboards in each room are filled with books and knickknacks: the little brown and white Inuit figure I bought for Mom when I was fourteen, the carved and painted figures from one of my brother's travels to Quebec. A big box of toys crowds one wall, awaiting the visits of numerous grandchildren. Dad's ancient slide projector and his boxes of slides recording years of holidays and birthdays stack the shelves in the TV room closet. This room used to be my parents' bedroom. I remember sneaking in here during the night to cuddle with Mom, hoping Dad wouldn't wake up and send me back to bed, when I was afraid of the faces the shadows made in the patterned curtains.

In my old room, I sit for a moment on the edge of the double bed. Trevor and I slept here after our accident. We sleep here still when we visit, always with a playpen set up at the end of the bed.

I know Mom has to move on. She's getting older, and the house and yard are too much for her. This house has been a source of security and warmth in my troubled life. For her, it's been her life. I am filled with an intense yearning and sense of loss. Why do things have to change?

I lift the portable phone on the bedside table to call home. *My* home, hundreds of miles away, where new young lives are being enacted. Another family of children crawling into bed with their parents in the small hours of the morning. Another couple struggling to feel love and to give it, to listen to the stories their children tell. Will Trevor and I get old there, as we planned? Will we be deciding what to pack for a move to a smaller house one day?

❧

I'm back in the hospital again, in the old building just down the hill behind our house. I lie inert, bed curtains pulled around me. For weeks I have tried to shove this descent away. My head is thick with despair.

Dr. King comes in, still wearing his ski suit after a day on the slopes. "When you feel like this, you can't even remember what it is to be well. Am I right?"

Behind hands shielding my face from the world, I nod.

"You are a good person," he says.

I think and sleep and think and sleep. Nightmares of the bear stalking the hospital corridors wake me with a start in the night. After ten days, the tears come. My sobs are wrenching, and I am covered in perspiration.

My nurse, Cara, sits on a chair at my bedside. She strokes my arm, moves her hand over my damp shoulders and back. "Something is really bothering you," she says. She stays with me as time passes.

Slowly my words come, choked and thick. "Tell them I'm sorry. I'm so, so sorry." I cry and cry, but at the end I am still, peaceful.

The day before my discharge, Trevor comes with the children to my hospital room, bringing a thermos of tea and a bag of raisin cookies. He leans against the wall as the children cluster on the bed, one under each of my arms and two sitting near my feet. We eat and drink, talk and argue and laugh.

I am home from the hospital for only a day and a half when I am readmitted. The facial infection has returned, after two years without it. The left side of my face is swollen and hot inside. I feel ill and so tired I cannot stay awake. When I hug Trevor and the children good-bye I try to make light of the possibilities, but I am so afraid. This may indicate a recurrence of abscess or a bone infection.

As so many times before, I lie alone in my hospital bed in the dark of night, wrestling with fear and horrible images. Fever and pain render me immobile through a succession of anaesthetics, incisions, drugs, green-masked faces.

No. I will not let the terror wrap me in its ugly grasp.

My family doctor arranges for a portable IV pump so that I can finish the antibiotic therapy as an outpatient. I will have to carry the six-by-six–inch machine in a fanny pack for two weeks, twenty-four hours a day, changing the medication bags myself and visiting the hospital for tubing and needle changes. By now the drugs have a grip on the infection, and my pain and illness have lessened. I jump back into life with both feet.

The phone rings with requests. Could I come to a meeting of consumers and caregivers at the Mental Health offices? Would I be willing to address local police about the needs of mental-health consumers? Would I give my comments on the building of a lock-up room in our local hospital? Napier's search and rescue team ask Trevor and me to talk to them about our attack. AboutFace wonders if I can write a piece for its newsletter.

I search out unfinished house projects. After a year and a half of seeing the fabric for bathroom curtains folded and waiting beside the tub, I sew them up, and cabbage roses now filter the sunlight. I make an appointment for a makeover. I will get my hair cut too, maybe tinted. And I want to cheer up my wardrobe with some new spring colour.

But Will is clinging, and he cries whenever I leave him. Ellen is frightened of the pump, requiring constant reassurance that it does not hurt me, that I will not die. Daniel wants me to help at his school, as his friends' parents do; I volunteer to work with students on their reports about wild animals. Nicola is slated to perform three violin pieces in the upcoming arts festival, and I become her audience during early-morning rehearsals. Trevor works long hours. He and I visit late at night while the world sleeps.

The pump flashes messages across its screen and beeps incessantly. I wear the awkward box wherever I go, embarrassing my children with the urine-coloured tubing that transports liquid, stopping to push buttons in the middle of a downtown street, changing the bag of medication at the playground with Will. The bear reenters my dreams as once again I battle pain where my face was torn apart.

I force myself to sit at the computer and pour my heart out rather than going back to bed to hide. Oenone stays with the children while I write. When I come downstairs one afternoon, she is putting her coat on. Her lovely face smiles my way as she swings her hair out of her eyes and slides into her boots.

"Hi, Trish. We made a batch of cookies today. Will only slept for an hour. Ellen had a quiet time, but she didn't sleep. Trevor's upstairs having a nap."

"Thanks. See you tomorrow."

Daniel chases her to the door with a squirt gun. I turn from the noise of their wrestling to the patio doors in our dining room, and I feel my heart lift at the sunshine pouring in on this late winter day. Ellen has wrapped herself around my waist, chiming, "Could I have a hug, Mom? Could I have a hug?" Her brown hair is pulled into erratic small ponytails on her head. I bend to return her hug and to lift Will into my arms.

"Hey. Everyone! Who wants to dance?"

At the stereo, I place Daniel's favourite Enya disk in the machine, and the music fills the room. Holding Will tightly, I swivel and step. He laughs with pleasure. Daniel dips and spins. Ellen, a scarf from the toy box draped over her head, happily traces the designs in the carpet with her feet. I go back to the machine and turn it up loud. Trevor and Nicola come down the stairs, looking quizzical. Nicola has been playing with makeup. She joins us, twisting her slender body and smiling at me with dark purple lips and deep, blue-shadowed eyes. Trevor takes Will. As the music speeds up, we all join hands in a circle and turn faster and faster.

❦

I am forty and looking at it in the mirror. Mountains and a sea of evergreens are reflected in the glass from the window behind me.

I consider my patched face, one blue eye, brown hair, small smile with a bit of overbite. Beautiful, strong, courageous;

disfigured, weak, cowardly: I have to see and decide for myself. I cover my left eye area and feel the warmth easing from hand to socket as I imagine richly coloured silk patches with maybe the glint of a gem in the corner.

I am alive and a part of this world. I have a loving partner and four beautiful children to share my journey. I am a survivor of illness, depression and a suicide attempt, of a savage anguish rendered voiceless by my fear of rejection. I am the survivor of a grizzly bear attack.

On a narrow ledge beside me is a tiny grizzly carved from turquoise. I take it down from time to time and hold it, running the tip of my finger over the minuscule hump on its back. I bought it after hearing how some believe a person attacked by a bear assumes that bear's wisdom and powers. Only now am I starting to know.

For seventeen years I have had a recurring nightmare. I am locked in a cage. There is a black opening at the back, and out of the opening comes a bear. I curl up tight, but still it comes. It claws at me and bites into my face, my neck, my head, with the sound of teeth scraping on bone. There is the smell of blood and fur and fear.

One night I have the dream again. I am locked in a cage. There is a black opening at the back. Out of the opening comes a bear. I am on my knees, hands clasped in front of me, and I beg the bear not to hurt me. I beseech it to leave me alone. I am too injured already. I can take no more. The bear approaches me and I cringe, preparing myself for the attack. But this time, its arms reach out to hold me close. It whispers comfort in my ear. I am held and rocked and cared for, safe in the bear's embrace.

Acknowledgements

Thank you to *all* of you who have been a part of this book
for your knowledge, faith and love, especially Barbara Pulling,
Bev Harris, Rita Moir, Theresa Kishkan, Kevin Van Tighem,
Carolyn Swayze, Rob Sanders and Trevor Janz.

And thank you too to Jean Vanier, whose writings
have inspired me to choose life.

PATRICIA VAN TIGHEM was born in Calgary, Alberta, where she began writing in her teens. Winner of a Canada Permanent Trust short-story competition, she was awarded a scholarship to the creative writing program at the Banff School of Fine Arts under the tutelage of the late W.O. Mitchell.

Patricia Van Tighem trained as a nurse at Mount Royal College and the University of Victoria. Until her death in December 2005, she lived with her family in a small town in the mountains of British Columbia.